A Guide to Syllogism, or, A Manual of Logic

...

A GUIDE TO SYLLOGISM,

OR,

A MANUAL OF LOGIC.

LONDON:
Printed by C. Richards, 100, St Martin's-lane, Charing-cross

A GUIDE TO SYLLOGISM,

.OR,

A MANUAL OF LOGIC;

COMPREHENDING

AN ACCOUNT OF THE MANNER OF DISPUTATION NOW
PRACTISED IN THE SCHOOLS AT CAMBRIDGE ;

WITH SPECIMENS OF THE DIFFERENT ACTS.

ADAPTED TO THE USE OF

THE HIGHER FORMS IN GRAMMAR SCHOOLS, AND OF
JUNIOR STUDENTS AT THE UNIVERSITY.

BY

THE REV. CHARLES WESLEY, B.D.

Late of Christ's College, Cambridge.

———————

" A Syllogism is a form of reasoning which serves to compress much
matter into a little compass, and helps to investigate truth with
certainty."—*Bishop Watson.*

———————

LONDON:

HENRY G. BOHN, 4, YORK STREET, COVENT-GARDEN;
DEIGHTON & SONS, CAMBRIDGE; J. PARKER, OXFORD.

———

M.DCCC.XXXII.

INTRODUCTION.

THE object of the compiler, in arranging these pages, is to lead the student, by the shortest path, to an acquaintance with the more interesting and practical parts of Logic. It appears to him, that there are many persons who would decline the perusal of a treatise on *Apprehension*, the *Divisions of Nouns*, and the different sorts of *Predicables*, who might be interested in examining the nature of Propositions, and the principle on which an Inference is conclusively drawn.

He is confirmed in this opinion, by having often observed, that youths of an ingenious and intellectual turn, disinclined as they might be to undertake the perusal of a bulky volume upon Logic, are generally gratified when an argument is set before them, in the brief and lucid form of a Syllogism.

The Appendix contains a summary account of the manner of syllogizing in the schools at Cambridge; and it is hoped that younger disputants, who are about to appear there, may derive some advantage from the following pages.

To the Regii Professors in Divinity, Law, and Physic, and to the Rev. Dr. Graham, Master of Christ's College, Cambridge, the compiler has to offer his most grateful thanks for the numerous obligations under which they have laid him.

He has the honour also to confess himself indebted to the learned and accomplished author* of the "Elements of Logic," not only for the advantage of his published writings, but for many acts of private courtesy.

* The present Archbishop of Dublin.

A GUIDE TO SYLLOGISM,

&c. &c.

OF REASONING AND SYLLOGISM.

1. An act of reasoning is performed by comparing two ideas together by means of a third, that must agree with *one* of them. If this third idea agrees with the other two, those two, of course, *agree* with one another; if it agrees with only one, they, of course, *disagree* with one another.*

2. A syllogism (from συλλογίζομαι, to reason) is an argument stated at full length, and in regular logical form.

3. By an argument's being stated at full length, is meant, that the application of the third idea to

---

* E. G. In reasoning on the character of Cæsar, if I wished to ascertain whether the idea of 'a good man' agreed with him, I might take, for a third idea, that of 'Tyrant.' On finding this *agree* with 'Cæsar,' and *disagree* with 'good man,' I should say that the ideas of 'Cæsar' and 'good man' *disagreed with one another ;* or, in other words, that 'Cæsar was not a good man.' The third idea, thus employed to assist us in forming a judgment, is called *a middle term.*

B

the two others is expressed in terms, and that however obvious the application may be, in the case of
one of them, it is never, on that account, taken for
granted.

4. By an argument's being stated in regular logical form, is meant, its being so arranged, that the
conclusiveness of it is manifest from the mere force
of the expression, *i. e.* without considering the
meaning of the terms. Thus,

> Every Y is X,
> Every Z is Y, therefore
> Every Z is X.

If you grant the two former assertions, (or premises,)
you cannot deny the conclusion.

5. Syllogisms are divided into Categorical,(from
κατηγορέω, I affirm,) and Hypothetical, (from ὑπό-
θεσις, a supposition.)   Categorical syllogisms are
divided into Pure and Modal ; hypothetical syllogisms into Conditional and Disjunctive. Syllogisms
take their names from the different kinds of propositions employed in forming them.

OF PROPOSITIONS.

6. A proposition is a sentence that affirms or
denies.   It consists of three parts, viz. the *subject,*

or thing spoken of; the *predicate*, or that which is said of it; and the *copula*, which must be the substantive verb, with or without a negative particle, as the subject and predicate happen to agree or disagree.

7. The subject and predicate are called Terms or Extremes,* because, according to logical order, the subject is placed first, the predicate last, and the copula in the middle.

Ex.—| *Subj.* | *Cop.* | *Pred.* |
| Vice | is | detestable. |

| *Subj.* | *Cop.* | *Pred.* |
| Virtue | is not | unrewarded. |

8. The substantive verb alone is recognized by logic; all other verbs are resolvable into the substantive verb with a participle or adjective.

Ex.—The summer approaches.

| *Subj.* | *Cop.* | *Pred.* |
| The summer | is | approaching. |

He does not know it.

| *Subj.* | *Cop.* | *Pred.* |
| He | is not | aware of it. |

9. As the copula is used merely to express the agreement or disagreement of the terms, it is, or

---

* In speaking of a syllogism, the term "extremes" is often understood to imply the extremes of the *conclusion*.

may be, always put in the present tense.   Should
the tense of the substantive verb modify the sense of
the proposition, this circumstance must be viewed
as part of one of the terms.*

Ex.—Troy *is* existent.

Troy *was* existent, *i. e.*—

Subj.	Cop.	Pred.
Troy	is	a place that was formerly existent.

10. An adjective or participle, though it cannot
be the subject, may yet be the predicate of a proposition; but even then a substantive appears to
be understood; as, " Life is short," " Art is long."
In these two propositions, the word " thing " may
be supplied to each predicate.—*See* SYNCATEGO-
REMATIC WORD, *in the Index.*

---

* The variety of expression allowable in language will
often occasion a proposition to appear in a form very different from that recognized by logic.   To that form, however, all propositions are reducible; and the pupil should
be accustomed to bring into it with readiness, propositions
of a dissimilar construction. E. G.

" Of his kingdom there shall be no end."

" An end of his kingdom is that which shall not be."

·' In loftiness of thought Homer surpasses Virgil."

" Homer is a poet who surpasses Virgil in loftiness of
thought."

" It is the duty of youth to reverence age."

" To reverence age is the duty of youth."

11. Propositions are either Categorical, (and sub-divided into Pure* and Modal,) or Hypothetical (and subdivided into Conditional and Disjunctive.) This division is according to *substance*. They are either Affirmative or Negative. This division is accord-ing to *quality (i. e.* the quality of the *expression.)* They are Universal or Particular. This division is according to *quantity.*†

---

* A pure proposition is sometimes called " propositio de inesse," because it simply states that the predicate is, or is not, (metaphysically,) in the subject.

† Another division of propositions is into Singular and Indefinite. A singular proposition is one of which the sub-ject is an individual, (either a proper name, a singular pro-noun, or a common noun with a singular sign.) E. G. "Cæ-sar overcame Pompey," " I am the person," "This fable is instructive." But as these propositions predicate of the *whole* of the subject, they fall under the rules that govern universals. It is to be observed, that if the subject of a proposition consist of a number of nouns *collectively* under-stood, so that they are viewed as *one single thing or body,* the proposition is *singular*. E. G. "All the books in Pto-lemy's library amounted to 200,000 volumes," *i. e. all to-together.* "Two and two make four." " Cæsar, Pompey, and Crassus, constituted the first Triumvirate." When the word *together* can be added to the subject of the proposition, or when the word *each* cannot be introduced, that proposi-tion is *singular.*

An indefinite proposition is one that has no sign of uni-versality or particularity affixed to it, but leaves us to

12. A categorical proposition declares a thing [κατηγορεῖ] absolutely, as "I love," or "I am loving." "Man is not infallible." These are *pure* categoricals, asserting *simply* the agreement and disagreement of subject and predicate. "The wisest man may possibly be mistaken." "A prejudiced historian will probably misrepresent the truth." These are *modal* categoricals, asserting the *manner* of the agreement and disagreement between subject and predicate.*

13. A hypothetical proposition consists of two or more categoricals, united by a conjunction called the Copula. It asserts, not absolutely but, under an hypothesis or condition: such propositions are denoted by the conjunctions used in stating them. E. G. "If man is fallible, he is imperfect." This

judge, from the nature of the connexion between the terms or Extremes, (No.7,) whether it should be reckoned as universal or particular. See No. 19.

* The modality of a proposition is usually considered to affect the copula. Logical writers have selected, as most worthy of remark, four modes of connexion between subject and predicate:—viz. necessary, possible, impossible, and contingent. E. G. "Man is necessarily an animal." "A globe may possibly consist of water." "It is impossible a man should be a stone." "John may, or may not, be learned."

is called a conditional proposition, denoted by the conjunction " if." " It is either day or night." This is a disjunctive hypothetical, and is denoted by the disjunctive conjunction " either."

14. An affirmative proposition is one of which the copula (No. 6.) is affirmative, A negative proposition is one of which the copula is negative. There is an example of each in No. 7.

15. A universal proposition is one of which the predicate is affirmed or denied of the *whole* of the subject. Its usual signs are "all," "every," "none," &c.;* or a universal proposition may have for its subject a proper name, or a common name with a singular sign.—See note to No. 11. E. G. "'All tyrants are miserable," "No miser is rich," " England is an island."—A particular proposition is one of which the predicate is affirmed or denied of only *part* of the subject. Its usual signs are " some,"

---

* To the signs of universality might be added " whoever," " each," " neither," " always," " every where," &c. To those of particularity, " a few," " not every," "sometimes," " somewhere," &c. There are some particular signs which make a near approach to a universal affirmative, as " many," " very many," "almost all," " by far the greater part," &c. Some, on the other hand, come very near to a universal negative, as " few," "very few," "scarcely any," &c.

" many," "few," " several," " most," and " all" or
" every," if the copula be negative. E. G. " Some
islands are fertile." " Many worthy men have to
complain of ill fortune." "Most men are fond of
novelty." " All tyrants (or some tyrants) are not
assassinated." " None but" means "some, and
those only," or " one person, thing, or object, and
that only:" it is, therefore, the sign of a particular,
or a singular, proposition.

DISTRIBUTION OF TERMS, SYMBOLS OF QUANTITY AND QUALITY, ETC.

16. In all universal propositions, the subject is
distributed; an expression which signifies that a
term is used in its fullest extent; that it stands for
all its Significates, or the several things which it signifies: so that there is not an individual to which
the common term is applicable, that it does not embrace.   As, in the example, " All tyrants are miserable," the common term includes Dionysius,
Phraates, Nero, and every individual who is a tyrant.   In all particular propositions, the subject is
undistributed ; it stands for only part of its significates, and the common term then embraces only a
part of the individuals to which it is applicable :—

as, in the example, "Some islands are fertile," the common term " island," though applicable to Iceland and all barren islands, does not embrace them.

17. There are four kinds of pure categorical propositions, distinguished by the symbols, A, E, I, O.

> Universal affirmative, A.
> Universal negative, E.
> Particular affirmative, I.
> Particular negative, O.

18. The connexion between the extremes of a proposition is Necessary, Impossible, or Contingent.

19. To determine whether an indefinite proposition should be viewed as particular or universal, we must look to the connexion between the extremes; *i. e.* we must consider of the subject and predicate, whether they *necessarily agree,* or *necessarily disagree,* or *may,* or *may not agree.* The nature of the connexion between the extremes is called the *matter* of the proposition. In necessary and in impossible matter, an indefinite is understood as a universal; as, " Birds have wings ;" *i. e. all.* " Birds are not quadrupeds ;" *i. e. none.* In contingent matter, *i. e.* where the terms sometimes agree and sometimes not, an indefinite is understood as a particular; as, " Food is necessary to

life ;"* *i. e. some kind of food.* "Birds sing ;" *i. e. some* birds sing. "Birds are not carnivorous ;" *i. e. some* birds are not, or, all are not.

20. The rules for distribution are these :—

1st. All universal propositions, and no particular, distribute the *subject*.

2nd. All negative, and no affirmative, the predicate.†

---

* The learner should observe that the term in question is "*a thing necessary to life,*" and not conclude, from the word " necessary," that the connexion between the terms " food " and " necessary to life" is a necessary connexion. It is *contingent ;* because *it happens* that there are kinds of food which are *not* necessary to life ; as *it happens* that there are birds which do *not* sing, and birds which *are* carnivorous. Whereas it *cannot happen* that *any* creature without wings, or that *any* quadruped, should be a bird. It is *necessary* that a creature should have wings to constitute it a bird, and *impossible* for a quadruped to be one.

† Thus the distribution or non-distribution of the s*ubject* of every proposition depends on its *quantity;* the distribution or non-distribution of the predicate, on its *quality :* and note further, that if, in an affirmative proposition, the whole of the predicate should agree with the subject, the circumstance is *accidental,* and not *implied* in the *form of expression.* In the propositions, "All men are rational animals," and "All men are animals," the form of expression is the same; but in the one instance, it so happens, that the whole of the predicate agrees with the subject, which is

21. Two propositions are said to be opposed, when, having the same subject and predicate, they yet differ in quantity, or quality, or both. (See Nos. 11, 14, 15.) The use of the rules of opposition is, that they immediately point out what we may infer with regard to the truth or falsity of any other proposition which has the same subject and predicate as the proposition before us, but differs from it either in quantity, or quality, or both.

22. There are four different kinds of opposition : —1st. between the two universals A and E, differing in quality only, and called *Contraries*. 2nd, between the two particulars I and O, differing also in quality only, and called *Subcontraries*. 3rd, between A and I, or E and O, differing respectively in quantity only, and called *Subalterns*. 4th, between A and O, or E and I, differing respectively both in quantity and quality, and called *Contradictories*.*

---

not the case in the other. " All rational animals are men," but "all animals are not men." In a just definition, the terms are always *exactly equivalent*, and therefore, *convertible*.

* Four things are requisite to form a just contradiction ; —viz. that we speak of the same thing 1st in the same sense ; 2nd, as to the same part ; 3rd, compared with the

23. The signs "no" and "none" imply both universality and negation; they are contradictory, therefore, to the *particular* sign with an *affirmative* copula. We cannot contradict "some are," by "all are not." E. G. "*Some* monarchs *are* tyrants," "*All* monarchs *are not* tyrants,"—which are subcontrary propositions, perfectly compatible, and both particular.

24. Of subaltern propositions, the universal is called *subalternans*, the particular, *subalternate*.

25. *In necessary matter, all affirmatives are true*, (as, "All islands are surrounded by water," "Some islands are surrounded by water,") *and negatives false*, (as; "No islands are surrounded by water," "Some islands are not surrounded by water.") *In impossible matter, all negatives are true*, (as, "No triangles are squares,"

---

same thing; 4th, existing at the same time. By omitting one of these conditions, *is* and *is not* may be compatible. E. G. The carcass of a man *is* and *is not* a man; for *it is* a dead man, *it is not* a living one. 2nd. Zoilus *is* and *is not* black; for his face *is* black, and his hair *is not* black, but red. 3rd. Socrates *has* and *has not* a full head of hair; for he *has*, if compared with Scipio, he *has not*, if compared with Xenophon. 4th. Nestor *is* and *is not* old; for *he is*, if you speak of his third age, *he is not*, if you speak of his first.

"Some triangles are not squares,") *and affirmatives false,* (as, "All triangles are squares," " Some triangles are squares.") *In contingent matter, all universals are false,* (as, " All islands are fertile," "No islands are fertile,") *and particulars true,* (as, " Some islands are fertile," " Some islands are not fertile.")

26. In contingent matter, contraries are *both false,* but never *both true;* subcontraries *both true,* but never *both false;* contradictories, always *one true* and *the other false.*

27.

MATTER.

	N.	L.	C.
	false.	true.	false.

	N.	L.	C.
	false.	true.	true.*

E.   Subalterns *differing only in quantity.*   O.

Contraries *differing only in quality.*

Subcontraries *differing only in quality.*

Contradic... Quality & quality.
Contradic... Quantity & Quality.
Differing both in Quantity & Quality.

A.   Subalterns *differing only in quantity.*   I.

MATTER.

	Necess.	Imposs.	Conting.
A.	true.	false.	false.

	N.	I.	C.
I.	true.	false.	true.

* The truth or falsity of propositions is here seen to depend on the matter. See No. 19. Propositions may be

28. In subalterns, the truth of the particular, or *subalternate,* follows from the truth of the universal, or *subalternans;* and the falsity of the universal from the falsity of the particular.* The opposition between contradictories is so perfect, (since they differ both in quantity and quality, see No. 22.) that if any proposition is true, we may be sure its contradictory is false; if false, its contradictory true, &c.

CONVERSION OF PROPOSITIONS.

29. A proposition is said to be *converted,* when the subject and predicate are made to exchange places, as, "No triangles are squares," "No squares are triangles." The use of conversion is to give a ready insight into what may be inferred from another proposition, that differs from the one before us, by the terms being transposed. This change in the position of the terms may be combined with that of the quantity, or quality, or both, or neither,

---

framed in A, E, I, O, on the following subjects, and adapted to the scheme by way of exemplification.

   N. That islands should be surrounded by water.

   I. That triangles should be squares.

   C. That islands are fertile.

   * If *all* islands are surrounded by water, it is plain that *some* must be so. If that *any one* triangle is a square be false, it must be false to say that *all* are so.

as the case may be.   By conversion, a facility is likewise afforded in effecting the reduction of syllogisms, a process that will presently be explained.

30. The above is an instance of *simple conversion;* the subject and predicate being merely transposed; but as this can be done only when the terms of a proposition are of *exactly the same extent,* two other methods are in use, which enable us to convert, consistently with truth, every proposition whatever:— viz. 1st. the limitation of the predicate of the Exposita, (or proposition given,) from universal to particular, which is called conversion *per Accidens,* or by Limitation; and 2ndly, the adding *not* to the predicate of the exposita, and then denying its agreement with the subject, which is called conversion by Negation or Contra-position. But in the case of O, (the particular negative,) conversion by negation is effected by joining the negative particle of the copula to the predicate of the exposita, and then transposing the terms, as if the proposition had been I.

31. No conversion is employed for any logical purpose, unless it be *illative; i. e. when the truth of the converse is implied* by the truth of the exposita. (No. 30.)

32. Conversion is then only illative, when *no*

term is distributed in the converse, which was not distributed in the exposita ; else, you would em-ploy a term *universally* in the converse, which, in the exposita, was used only *partially*. (For " distributed" see No. 16.)

33. The following examples will shew how every proposition (A, E, I, O,) may be illatively converted, by some one of the three methods above mentioned :—viz. 1st, simply ; 2nd, *per accidens*, or by limitation ; 3rd, by negation or contraposition. E, I, simply; for E distributes both terms, (No. 16, 20.) and I, neither (No. 16, 20.); they are, therefore, of exactly the same extent (No. 30.), and simply convertible.

(E) No triangles are squares ; therefore
　　No squares are triangles.

(I) Some islands are fertile places; therefore
　　Some fertile places are islands.

E, A, *per accidens*, or by limitation; E, because the predicate being distributed as well as the subject, and admitting, therefore, of the sign of universality, (as is shewn by simple conversion,) it must, as a universal, include the particular.

(E) No triangles are squares ; therefore—
　　Some squares are not triangles.

c

(which follows from the truth of the simple converse.)   A is converted *per accidens,* or by limitation ; because, since it does not distribute the predicate (No. 20.), that predicate will not admit of a universal sign, and therefore requires a particular one.

>   (A) All birds are animals ; therefore
>   Some animals are birds.

You could not say, " All animals are birds."

A, O, by negation ; A, because the subject agrees universally with the predicate ; so that what disagrees with the predicate cannot agree with the subject.*

>   (A) All birds are animals ; therefore
>   What are not animals are not birds.

O, because, since you consider it as I, neither term is distributed, and the process is that of simple conversion.

>   *Cop.*
>   (O) Some islands ⌈are not⌉ fertile places; (first

state this as I, by joining the negative to the pre-

---

* It is the same thing to *affirm* some attribute of the subject, and to *deny* the absence of it; thus (A) " All birds are animals," is equipollent to (E) " No birds are not-animals," which is of course simply convertible ; " What are not animals, are not birds."

dicate, thus, "Some islands are $\overline{\text{not-fertile-places}}$," *Pred.*)
therefore—

Some places-not-fertile are islands.

You could not infer from the exposita, ("Some islands are not fertile places,") that " Some fertile places are not islands." Such a converse, indeed, would *accidentally* be true, but it would not follow from the form of expression. This will be seen by substituting other terms. E. G.

Some men $\overline{\text{are not}}$ poets ; you cannot infer " Some poets are not men," but you *may* infer—

Some who are not poets are men.

34. To assist the memory in applying the two former methods of conversion, (viz. simple, and *per accidens*,) Aldrich, who does not notice conversion by negation, gives the following mnemonic line;

fEcI simpliciter, convertitur EvA per Acci.

For the last, we may say,

A sed, et O pariter, convertas usque Negando.

Or,

fAxO per Contra; sic fit conversio tota.

OF SYLLOGISMS.

35. The validity of a syllogism depends on this axiom of Aristotle, " Whatever is predicated of a

c 2

term distributed, (No. 16.) whether affirmatively or negatively, may be predicated in like manner of every thing contained under it." In the example at No. 4, X is predicated of Y distributed, and Z is contained under Y, *(i. e.* is its subject;) X is, therefore, truly predicated of Z.

36. There are two canons of pure categorical syllogisms; 1st, *Two terms that agree with one and the same third, agree with each other;* 2nd, *Two terms, of which one agrees and another disagrees with one and the same third, disagree with one another.* On the former of these canons rests the validity of *affirmative* conclusions; on the latter, of *negative.*

37. There are six rules for ascertaining whether the canons have been strictly observed or not.

Rule 1st. *Every syllogism has three, and only three, terms;* viz. the middle term, and the two terms of the conclusion, or question.* The *subject* of the conclusion is called the *minor term;*† its *predicate,* the *major term;* and the middle

---

* These are commonly called *Extremes.*

† Because generally of less extent than the major and middle terms.

term is that with which each of them is separately compared, in order to judge of their agreement or disagreement with each other.*

Rule 2nd. *Every syllogism has three, and only three, propositions;* viz. the *major premiss,* in which the *major term* is compared with the *middle;* the *minor premiss,* in which the *minor term* is compared with the *middle;* and the conclusion, in which the *minor term* is compared with the *major.*

Rule 3rd. *The middle term must not be ambiguous;*† which is the case whenever it is *equivocal,* or *undistributed.* An equivocal term is used in different senses in the two premises; E.G.

> " *Sage* is a plant;
>
> A philosopher is *sage;* therefore
>
> A philosopher is a plant."

If a term be undistributed, as it then stands for a *part* only of its significates, it may happen that one of the extremes may have been compared with one part of it, and the other with another part: E.G.

---

* If there were two middle terms, the extremes not being both compared with the *same,* could not be conclusively compared with each other.

† If the middle term is ambiguous, there are, in reality, two middle terms in *sense,* though but one in sound.

" Apples are fruit;
  Cherries are fruit; therefore
  Cherries are apples."

The middle term, therefore, must be distributed once, at least, in the premises; *i. e.* by being the subject of a universal, or predicate of a negative.

Rule 4th. *No term must be distributed in the conclusion, which was not distributed in one of the premises;* because you would then employ the whole of a term in the conclusion, when you had employed only a part of it in the premiss; and thus, in reality, introduce a fourth term. The violation of this fourth rule is called an *illicit process* of the major or minor term; E. G.

*" All apples are fruit;
  Cherries are not apples; therefore
  They are not fruit." Illicit process of the major.

" All beasts of prey are carnivorous;
†All beasts of prey are animals; therefore
All animals are carnivorous." Illicit process of the minor.

---

* This is A, and no affirmatives distribute the predicate. The conclusion is E, and all negatives *do* distribute the predicate. (No. 20.)

† This also is A, and does not distribute the predicate.

Rule 5th. *From negative premises you can infer
nothing;* for in them the middle term is pronounced to *disagree with both extremes,* not to
agree with both, or to agree with one and *disagree*
with the other: therefore they cannot be compared
together; E. G.

" A fish is not a quadruped;"

" A bird is not a quadruped,"* proves nothing.

Rule 6th. *If one premiss be negative, the conclusion must be negative;* for in that premiss the
middle term is pronounced to disagree with one of
the extremes, and in the other premiss, (which
must be affirmative by the preceding rule,) to agree
with the other extreme; therefore, the extremes
disagreeing with each other, the conclusion is negative. To prove a negative conclusion, one of the
premises must be negative.†

"animals." The conclusion again is A, and *does* distribute
the *subject,* "animals."

* In order to shew the disagreement between the terms
"fish" and "bird," you must choose a middle term that
agrees with one of them. E. G. "A feathered creature is
not a fish; a bird is a feathered creature; therefore," &c.
Or, "No animal that inhabits the water is a bird; a fish is
an animal that inhabits the water; therefore," &c.

† To prove that the sun is not a planet, you must not

38. From these rules it is evident, first, that*
*nothing can be proved from two particular pre-
mises;* and secondly,† that *if one of the premises
be particular, the conclusion must be particular.*‡

---

take for a middle term "sphere," which agrees with both,
but a middle term that disagrees either with "sun" or
"planet." E. G. "Every planet describes an orbit; the
sun does not describe an orbit; therefore it is not a planet."
Or, "The sun is a fixed star; a planet is not a fixed star;
therefore it is not the sun."

* You will then have either the middle term undistributed, or an illicit process. E. G. "Some animals are sagacious; some beasts are sagacious; therefore, some beasts
are animals." Undistributed middle. This conclusion is
true, but does not follow from the premises. The argument
is of the same construction as the following absurdity:
"Some animals are black; some hats are black; therefore,
some hats are animals." Again, "Some animals are sagacious; some beasts are not sagacious; therefore, some
beasts are not animals." Here is an illicit process of the
major. "Some carnivorous creatures are tame; some beasts
are not tame; therefore, no beasts are carnivorous creatures." This exhibits an illicit process of both the major
and minor term.

† E. G. "All who fight bravely deserve reward; some
soldiers fight bravely; therefore, some soldiers deserve reward." If you were to infer, "All soldiers deserve, &c."
there would be an illicit process of the minor.

‡ The following mnemonic lines, from Aldrich, may assist the student in applying these rules and remarks;

39. From universal premises you cannot always infer a universal conclusion; E. G. " All gold is precious; all gold is a mineral; therefore some mineral is precious." But when you *can* infer a universal, you are always *at liberty* to infer a particular.

OF MOODS.

40. The mood of a syllogism is the designation of it according to the quantity (No. 11.) and quality (No. 11.) of each of its three propositions, which are denoted by the vowels A, E, I, O, (No. 17.). There are only eleven moods admissible, as conforming to the rules laid down at No. 37. *See No. 44, below.*

OF FIGURES.

41. The figure of a syllogism indicates the situ-

Distribuas medium (Rule 3.), nec quartus terminus adsit; (Rule 1 & 2.)

Utraque nec præmissa negans (Rule 5.), nec particularis; (No. 38.)

Sectetur partem Conclusio deteriorem; (Rule 6,& No. 38.)

Et non distribuat, nisi cum præmissa, negetve. (Rule 4 & 6.)

Logicians have attached to universal propositions an imaginary superiority over particulars, and to affirmatives a similar superiority over negatives. Hence the expression " pars deterior," meaning a particular or a negative proposition.

ation of the middle term with regard to the extremes of the conclusion, or *major and minor term.* (No. 37, Rule 1, and Note.) There are four figures.* In the first, the middle term is made *the subject of the major premiss, and the predicate of the minor:* in the second, the middle term is the *predicate of both premises:* in the third, *the subject* of both: in the fourth, it is *the predicate of the major premiss, and the subject of the minor.*

42. The major premiss of a syllogism is usually placed first, although, of course, the validity of the argument is not affected by the order of the two premises.

43. Each of the moods alluded to in No. 40, as admissible, will not be so in every figure; since, from the different position of the middle term, it may violate some of the foregoing rules in one figure, though not in another.†

---

* The first figure is the most natural and clear, and is at once open to the application of Aristotle's dictum. (No.35.) The last is, in all respects, the very reverse of the first.

† I, A, I, for instance, is allowable in the third figure; because, in that figure, the middle term is made the subject of both the major and minor premiss. (No. 41.) It is, therefore, regularly distributed in the minor proposition A, (No. 20,) and as *neither* term is distributed in the conclusion I,

44. Although but eleven moods were stated to be admissible at No. 40, yet, since some of them occur in more than one figure, (as E, I, O, which

---

(No. 16, 20,) there can be no illicit process. (No. 37.) But I, A, I, is inadmissible in the first figure, because that figure demands that the middle term be made the subject of the major proposition I, and the predicate of the minor A. But I distributes neither term, and A, only the subject. (No. 20.) The middle term, therefore, being the subject of a particular, and the predicate of an affirmative, would be undistributed, contrary to rule, and no valid conclusion could follow. E. G.

I. Some arrogant men are learned;

A. All arrogant men are disagreeable; therefore

I. Some learned men are disagreeable.

The above is in the third figure, and valid. In the first figure, the same mood would be inadmissible, for the reasons above stated. E. G.

I. Some learned men are Englishmen;

A. The sages of Greece were learned men; therefore

I. Some of them were Englishmen.

So A, E, E, would, in the first figure, have an illicit process of the major; thus

A. Every fool is a sensualist;

E. No true philosopher is a fool; therefore

E. No true philosopher is a sensualist.

The major term, "sensualist," is not distributed in the major proposition, but is, in the conclusion. The same mood, in the second figure, is valid, because the major term "sensualist" is regularly distributed in the major proposition; E. G.

is found in all the four,*) each separate occurrence
is reckoned as a new mood. From this recurrence
of the same symbols in different figures, there are
reckoned nineteen moods.

    A. Every sensualist is a fool ;
    E. No true philosopher is a fool ; therefore
    E. No true philosopher is a sensualist.

Again, A, A, A, is allowable in the first figure ;

    A. All wicked men are miserable ;
    A. All tyrants are wicked men ; therefore
    A. All tyrants are miserable.

But, in the third figure, it would have an illicit process
of the minor ;

    A. All wicked men are miserable ;
    A. All wicked men are tyrants ; therefore
    A. All tyrants are miserable.

The minor term, "tyrants," is not distributed in the minor premiss ; but is, in the conclusion.

*A A A. *Barbara.*	A O O. *Fakoro.*
A A I. *Darapti* Bramantip.	E A E. *Cesare, Celarent.*
A E E. *Camestres,Camenes.*	E A O. *Felapton, Fesapo.*
A E O.	E I O. *Ferio, Festino, Feriso*
A I I. *Darii, Datisi.*	*Fresison.*
I A I. *Disamis, Dimaris.* ·	O A O. *Dokamb.*

A, E, O, is valid in the second figure, but useless, because it has a particular conclusion when you *might* draw a
universal one in *Camestres.* E. G. (A.) Every X is Y. (E.)
No Z is Y. (O.) Some Z is not X. You *might* say, *No Z*
is X. (A.) "Every man is a sinner. (E.) No glorified spirit is a sinner. (O.) Some glorified spirit is not a man."

45. The vowels in the four following mnemonic lines are the symbols which denote the quantity and quality of the propositions. The consonants serve to keep in mind the figure of the syllogism.

Fig. 1. Barbara, Celarent, Darii, Ferioque prioris;

Fig. 2. Cesare, Camestres, Festino, Fakoro, secundæ;

Fig. 3. Tertia, Darapti, Disamis, Datisi, Felapton, Dokamo, Feriso, habet; quarta insuper addit

Fig. 4. Bramantip, Camenes, Dimaris, Fesapo, · Fresison.

46. It will assist the experiment of syllogisms in the different moods, if the letters X, Y, Z, are used as representatives of the different terms. Let X be the major, Y the middle, Z the minor.

SCHEME.

1st Fig.	2nd Fig.	3rd Fig.	4th Fig.
Y, X,	X, Y,	Y, X,	X, Y,
Z, Y,	Z, Y,	Y, Z,	Y, Z,
Z, X,	Z, X,	Z, X,	Z, X.

You *might* say, "No glorified spirit," &c. The same may be remarked of A, A, I, and E, A, O, in the first figure, and of E, A, O, in the second, as well as of A, E, O, in the fourth. See No. 39. These five moods, being useless, are without names.

By applying the moods *Barbara, Celarent, &c.*
to the terms thus designated by the letters X, Y, Z,
you may construct a short syllogism in every figure, and perceive how its validity is derived from
an accordance with the six rules laid down above.
No. 37.*

---

* Thus *Barbara*, in which all the propositions are universal and affirmative, as the three A's denote.

Bar- "Every Y is X;
-ba-   Every Z is Y;
-ra.   Every Z is X."

Celarent, in which the major is universal and negative,
the minor universal and affirmative, and the conclusion
universal and negative.

Ce-   "No Y is X;
-la-   Every Z is Y;
-rent. No Z is X."

Darii, in which the major is universal and affirmative,
the minor particular and affirmative, and the conclusion
the same.

Da-   "Every Y is X;
-ri-   Some Z is Y;
-i.   Some Z is X."

Ferio, in which the major is universal and negative, the
minor particular and affirmative, and the conclusion particular and negative.

Fe-   "No Y is X;
-ri-   Some Z is Y;
-o.   Some Z is not X.

Apply the other moods *Cesare Camestres*, &c. in the same
way to the second figure; *Darapti*, &c. to the third; Bra

. 47.* Every proposition may be proved in the first figure, and all the moods in the three other figures reduced to it. See No. 53 *et seq.* below.

48. Four syllogisms, exemplifying one mood in each figure, are subjoined.

---

mant*ip*, &c. to the fourth; carefully remembering the force of the symbols A, E, I, O, (No. 17.) The position of the Letters X, Y, Z, in the scheme, secures the learner against any mistake in placing the terms of each figure.

* It will be seen that A, or the universal affirmative, can be proved only in the first figure; as the second proves only negatives, (E, E, O, O,) the third only particulars, (I, I, I, O, O, O,) and the fourth only particulars or negatives. (I, E, I, O, O.) The first figure requires the major premiss to be universal, and the minor affirmative; the former, in order to distribute the middle term, and the latter, to avoid the fault of negative premises, (No. 37. Rule 5.) or to produce an affirmative conclusion. (No. 37. Rule 6.) The second figure proves only negatives, because the middle term, being the predicate in both premises, would not be distributed, unless one premiss were negative, (No. 20. Rule 2.) and therefore the conclusion must be negative. (No. 37. Rule 6.) The third proves only particulars, because the middle term being always the subject in the minor proposition, and that minor proposition being always affirmative, the minor term, as the predicate of an affirmative, cannot be distributed in its premiss, and therefore cannot be distributed in the conclusion.

Barbara. *Fig.* 1.

TERMS.

Major (X) One who deserves punishment.

Minor (Z) Every blasphemous writer.

Middle (Y) Every one who injures the public morals.

Bar- Every Y is X; All who injure the public morals deserve punishment;

-ba- Every Z is Y; All blasphemous writers injure the public morals; therefore

-ra. Every Z is X; All blasphemous writers deserve punishment.*

---

* The regular expression of the copula, *is* and *is not*, may always be preserved, if we disregard the clumsiness of the language; thus, the syllogism above may be stated as follows:

Bar- All who injure the public morals *are* persons deserving of punishment;

-ba- All blasphemous writers *are* persons who injure the public morals; therefore

-ra. All blasphemous writers *are* persons deserving of punishment.

Pupils should be able to state a proposition readily in this strict form.

49.   Camestres.   *Fig.* 2. .

Major (X) What is truly satisfactory.

Minor (Z) Guilty pleasures.

Middle (Y) What is unattended with remorse.

Cam- Every X is Y; Whatever is truly satisfac-
    tory is unattended with remorse;

-es- No Z is Y; No guilty pleasures are unat-
    tended with remorse; therefore

-tres. No Z is X. No guilty pleasures are truly
    satisfactory.

50.   Darapti.   *Fig.* 3.

Major (X) What is entitled to respect.

Minor (Z) What is often ridiculed.

Middle (Y) True piety.

Da- Every Y is X; True piety is entitled to re-
    spect;

-rap- Every Y is Z; True piety is often ridi-
    culed; therefore

-ti. Some Z is X. Something often ridiculed
    is entitled to respect.

D

51.   Camenes.   Fig. 4.

TERMS.

Major (X) A useful study.

Minor (Z) What is injurious to the morals.

Middle (Y) What is worthy of encouragement.

Cam- Every X is Y; All useful studies are worthy
        of encouragement;

-en- No Y is Z; Nothing worthy of encourage-
        ment is injurious to the morals; therefore

-es. No Z is X. What is injurious to the mo-
        rals is not a useful study.*

52. The four moods of the first figure are called
fect; all the rest, *imperfect.* When a syllogism
in one of the imperfect moods is re-stated, and
brought into the first figure, it is said to be *reduced.*

OSTENSIVE REDUCTION.

53. In reducing a syllogism, it is allowable to
convert the premises illatively, (No. 31,) or to
transpose them. This liberty renders it always
possible to deduce, in the first figure, either the very
same conclusion as the original one, or another,
from which the original one is deducible by illative
conversion.

---

* The method of statement in this figure is so clumsy
and inverted, that it is seldom or never used. The propo-

54. The initial letters of the imperfect moods correspond with those of the four perfect ones, B, C, D, F, and indicate into which of them the imperfect mood is capable of being reduced. Thus *Bramantip* is to be reduced into *Barbara, Cesare* and *Camestres* into *Celarent, Festino* into *Ferio, &c.*

55. The letter *m,* occurring in the name of an imperfect mood, indicates that, in reducing it, the premises are to be transposed ; *s,* that the proposition denoted by the vowel immediately preceding, is to be *converted simply* (No. 33.); *p,* that it is to be *converted per accidens* or limitation (No. 30.); (except in the case of *Bramantip,* where *p* denotes that the conversion of A *per accidens* has *already* taken place ;*) *k,* that it is to be *converted* by *negation.* (No. 30.)†

---

sitions are easily reduced into the more natural arrangement of the first figure. See No. 54.

   * E. G. Bram- All blasphemous writers injure the public morals ;

        -an- All who injure the public morals deserve punishment ; therefore

        -tip. Some who deserve punishment are blasphemous writers.

The conclusion is the converse *per accidens* of the conclusion of the Syllogism in Barbara, No. 48.

   † The *Reductio ad impossibile* I have not thought it ne-

56. A few examples of reduction may suffice :
Camestres is reduced to *Celarent,* as the initial letter directs, by simply converting the minor, (as
is denoted by the *s* in *es,*) and then transposing
the premises, (as is indicated by the *m* in *Cam.)*
The conclusion of the reduced syllogism is the
simple converse of the conclusion of the original
one.

CAMESTRES. *See No.* 49.
Reduced to CELARENT.

Ce- What is unattended with remorse is not a
    guilty pleasure ;

-la- Whatever is truly satisfactory is unattended
    with remorse ; therefore

-rent. Whatever is truly satisfactory is not a guilty
    pleasure.

57. *Fakoro* is reduced to *Ferio* by converting
the major by negation, (No. 30.) and considering

---

cessary to explain. Its object is, to show that an absurdity
would follow from supposing the original conclusion to be
false. When this mode of reduction is adopted, *Fakoro*
and *Dokamo* are called *Baroko* and *Bokardo,* K being then
the sign of the *Reductio ad impossibile.* But conversion
by negation is by far the easier and more expeditious
process.

the minor premiss affirmative; *i. e.* attaching the negative to the predicate instead of the copula. (No. 30.)

Fakoro.
Reduced to Ferio.

Fak- Every sincere Christian is charitable;

-o-   Some professors of religion are not charitable; therefore

-ro.   Some professors of religion are not sincere Christians.

Fe-   He who is not-charitable is not a sincere Christian.

                                                Predicate.

-ri-   Some professors of religion are $\overline{\text{not-charitable;}}$ therefore

-o.   Some professors of religion are not sincere Christians.*

---

   * *Fakoro* may be considered as *Festino*, and stated accordingly, by placing an equipollent negative Proposition for the major, (No. 33, Note,) and viewing the minor as an affirmative.

           Subject.   *Predicate.*

Fes- $\overline{\text{No sincere Christian}}$ is $\overline{\text{not-charitable;}}$

                                 Predicate

-ti- Some professors of religion are $\overline{\text{not-charitable;}}$ therefore

-no. Some professors of religion are not sincere Christians.

The minor premiss is here considered affirmative, because you take "not-charitable" as the middle
term, and cannot separate the negative from it,
without introducing a fourth term, contrary to No.
37, Rule 1.

58. *Darapti* is reduced to *Darii* by converting
per accidens (No. 30.) the minor premiss.   This
is denoted by the *p* in *rap*. (No. 55.)

Festino is reduced to *Ferio* by simply converting the major; " He who is not charitable is not a sincere Christian,"
&c.

So *Dokamo* may be considered as *Disamis*, and stated
accordingly, by joining the negative to the predicate instead of the copula, in the major and conclusion; *i. e.* viewing O as I;

Predicate.

Dis-   Some desires are | not-blameable; |

-am- All desires are liable to excess; therefore

Predicate.

-is.   Some things liable to excess are | not-blameable. |

Disamis is reduced to *Darii* by simply converting the
major, and then transposing the premises.

Da- All desires are liable, &c.

-ri- Some things not blameable, &c.; therefore

-i. Some things not blameable, &c. as at No. 59.

DARAPTI. *See No.* 50.
Reduced to DARII.

Da- True piety is entitled to respect;

-ri- Something often ridiculed is true piety; therefore

-i. Something often ridiculed is entitled to respect.

59. *Dokamo* is reduced to *Darii* by converting the major by negation, and then transposing the premises.

DOKAMO.
Reduced to DARII.

Dok- Some desires are not blameable;

-am- All desires are liable to excess; therefore

-o. Some things liable to excess are not blameable.

Da- All desires are liable to excess;

-ri- Some things not blameable are desires; therefore

-i. Some things not blameable are liable to excess.

This conclusion is the converse by negation of the original one, (*i. e.* O converted into I,) and therefore, simply convertible into it. (No. 33.)

60. Those syllogisms are called Modal, that consist of modal propositions. (No. 12.) Modal propositions may be considered as pure categoricals, and stated accordingly. For this purpose, you should attach the mode to one of the terms; as, " The wisest man may possibly be mistaken."

Subj.	*Cop.*	*Pred.*
" The wisest man	is	one who may possibly be mistaken."

" It is probable that Livy was prejudiced; *i. e.*

Subj.	*Cop.*	*Pred.*
"Livy	was	probably prejudiced."

61. When the mode expresses only the necessary, impossible, or contingent connexion of the terms, you may attach it to the *subject,* as " Man is *necessarily* mortal;" *i. e.* "*All* men are mortal." " It is *impossible* for a bad man to be happy;" *i.e.* "*No* bad man can be happy."

62. It is often, however, most convenient to affirm simply the agreement or disagreement of the mode with the dictum, or assertion itself; as " I am possibly mistaken,"

Subj.	*Cop.*	*Pred.*
" That I am mistaken	is	possible."

In these cases, the subject implies that an entire act of judgment has previously taken place.

OF HYPOTHETICAL SYLLOGISMS.

63. A syllogism is called Hypothetical, when it contains one, two, or three hypothetical propositions;   E. G. "If he is wise, he is happy; he is wise; therefore he is happy." Or, " He who is wise, is happy; if he is a philosopher, he is wise; therefore, if he is a philosopher, he is happy." Or, " If he is wise, he is happy; if he is a philosopher, he is wise; therefore, if he is a philosopher, he is happy." See No. 13. The hypothetical syllogisms most in use are divided into Conditional and Disjunctive. E. G.

CONDITIONAL.

If man is fallible, he is imperfect;
But he is fallible; therefore
He is imperfect.

DISJUNCTIVE.

It is either day or night;
But it is day; therefore
It is not night.

64. In a hypothetical syllogism, the reasoning

turns on the hypothesis, and the conclusion is always categorical.*

The hypothetical premiss is called the major, and the categorical one, the minor.

OF CONDITIONAL SYLLOGISMS.

65. It is to be observed of a conditional proposition, that it contains two, and only two, categorical propositions, whereof one results from the other; that from which the other results is called the Antecedent;* that which results from it, the Consequent *(Consequens.)* The connexion between the two (expressed by "if") is called the Consequence (*consequentia.*)

| *Consequentia.* | *Antecedent.* | *Consequent.* |

"If man is fallible, he is imperfect."

66. The truth or falsity of a conditional proposition depends entirely on the *consequence*, or *con-*

---

* When a hypothetical conclusion is drawn from a hypothetical premiss, the reasoning is, in effect, categorical. E.G.

Predicate.

Every conqueror is either a hero or a villain;
Cæsar was a conqueror; therefore

Predicate.

He was either a hero or a villain.

* The antecedent is sometimes placed *after* the consequent. We might say, "Man is imperfect, if he is fallible."

nexion between antecedent and consequent. Both
antecedent and consequent may be false, yet if
there be such a connexion between them, that the
falsity* of the antecedent *depends* on the falsity of
the consequent, the whole proposition is valid.
E. G.

Antecedent.

If logic is useless,

Consequent.

 it deserves to be neglected.

On the other hand, both antecedent and consequent
may be *true;* yet if there be no connexion between
them, so that the latter does not depend for its
truth on the former, the whole proposition is *false;*
i. e. the consequent does *not follow* from the antecedent.

Antecedent.

If Virgil was a poet,

Consequent.

 he wrote the Æneid.

It is true both that Virgil was a poet, and that he

---

* If you deny the consequent, "Logic deserves to be neglected," the falsity of the antecedent, "Logic is useless,"
must follow. This will appear from a categorical statement
of the proposition. (A) "Whatever is useless is deserving
of neglect." Convert this by negation. (E) "Whatever
is not deserving of neglect is not useless. (No. 30.) Logic
is not deserving of neglect; therefore it is not useless."

wrote the Æneid, but it does not follow that *because*
he was a poet, he *therefore* wrote the Æneid.

67. There are two rules for drawing a conclusion from a conditional proposition. Rule 1. *The
antecedent being granted, the consequent may be
inferred*; E. G.

"If A is B, C is D; Major. "If rain has fallen, the
                                      ground is wet;

But A is B;   Minor. But rain has fallen;
   therefore   therefore

C is D."   Conclusion. The ground is wet."

These syllogisms, in which the antecedent is
granted, are called *Constructive*.

Rule 2. *The consequent being denied, the antecedent may be denied.*

"If A is B, C is D;   "If rain has fallen, the
                                    ground is wet;

But C is not D; therefore But the ground is not
                                    wet; therefore

A is not B."   Rain has not fallen."

These syllogisms, in which the consequent is denied,
are called *Destructive*.

68. By *denying* the *antecedent*, or *affirming* the
consequent, nothing can be inferred, because the
same consequent may follow from *other* antece-

dents. *Rain may not have fallen, and yet the ground may be wet; or †the ground may be wet, and yet no rain have fallen; because dew or an inundation would produce the same effect.‡

OF DISJUNCTIVE SYLLOGISMS.

69. To what has been said of a disjunctive pro-

---

* Here the antecedent is denied.

† Here the consequent is affirmed.

‡ Conversion by negation (No. 30) is applicable to conditional propositions; *i. e.* the contradictory of the consequent may be taken for the antecedent, and the contradictory of the antecedent for the consequent.

" If rain has fallen, the ground is wet;
  But rain has fallen; therefore   } Constructive.
  The ground is wet."

" If the ground is not wet, rain has not fallen;
  But rain has fallen; therefore   } Destructive.
  The ground is wet."

By this conversion of the major premiss of a constructive syllogism, (the minor, of course, remaining unchanged,) you will reduce a constructive syllogism into a destructive, because you deny the consequent. You will reduce a destructive syllogism into a constructive, because you affirm the antecedent. E. G.

" If rain has fallen, the gound is wet;
  But the ground is not wet; therefore } Destructive.
  Rain has not fallen."

" If the ground is not wet, rain has not fallen;
  But the ground is not wet; therefore } Constructive
  Rain has not fallen."

sition (No. 13) must be added, that it consists of
two or more categoricals so stated, as to imply that
some one of them, at least, is true, and generally
that *but one* can be true; as, "It is either day or
night."

70. By denying one of the categoricals of a disjunctive proposition, if there be but two, you may
infer the truth of the remaining one; as, "It is
either day or night: but it is not day; therefore
it is night." By denying one of them, if there be
several, you may infer the truth of *some one* of the
remaining ones; as, " It is either Spring, Summer,
Autumn, or Winter; but it is not Spring; therefore it is either Summer, Autumn, or Winter.'
By denying all but one, you will infer the truth of
that one; as, "It is neither Spring, Summer, nor
Autumn; therefore it is winter."

71. When it is implied that only one of the categoricals can be true, by *affirming* one, you, of
course, deny the rest. As, "It is either Spring,
Summer, &c.; but it is Spring; therefore it is neither Summer, Autumn, nor Winter."*

---

* If *both* categoricals should be true, it is plain that the
affirmation of one cannot imply the denial of the other; as,
"Amphibious creatures live either on land or in the water."

72. The dilemma* is a redundant conditional syllogism, with two or more antecedents in the major premiss, and a disjunctive minor.

73. Dilemmas are either Constructive or Destructive. Of the constructive dilemma there are two sorts, *Simple* and *Complex*. There is but one sort of the true destructive dilemma.

74. The simple constructive dilemma has but *one consequent* to each antecedent. The antecedents being disjunctively granted, in the minor, the common consequent is inferred. See No. 67. Rule

Major.

1. "If A is B, C is D; and if E is F, C is D.

Minor.	*Conclusion.*
But either A is B, or E is F;	therefore C is D."

"If a Christian be living, he is the Lord's servant; and if he be dead, he is the Lord's servant; but he

---

* As, in this kind of argument, there are generally, in the major premiss, two antecedents, which, in the minor, become two assùmptions, it is termed a *dilemma*, from δις *twice, two*, and λῆμμα, *an assumption*. It is called by the lexicographers, "Syllogismus ab utrâque parte feriens adversarium," and "Argumentum cornutum," because most horned animals have *two horns*, and there are, in a dilemma, *two instruments of attack*, furnished in the two assumptions. So Cowley, "Both the horns of fate's dilemma wound."

must be always either living or dead; therefore he is always the Lord's servant." (See *Romans*, xiv. 8.)*

75. The complex constructive dilemma has a different consequent to each antecedent. The antecedents are disjunctively granted, in the minor, and the different consequents disjunctively inferred.

Major.

E.G. "If A is B, C is D, and if E is F, G is H;

Minor.   *Con-*

but either A is B, or E is F;   therefore either

clusion.

C is D, or G is H." "If the Evangelists speak truth, Christianity is of God, and if they do not speak truth, the existence of Christianity is perfectly unaccountable; but the Evangelists either do or do not speak truth; therefore Christianity is either of God, or its existence is perfectly unaccountable."

76† The true destructive dilemma has, like the

---

* The conditionals of the major premiss may be united by the adverb "whether," so as to form one proposition; E. G. "Whether a Christian lives or dies, he is the Lord's servant."

† There is a form of argument incorrectly styled a destructive dilemma, in which the consequents are *wholly*

complex constructive, a different consequent to each
antecedent, in the major. The consequents are
disjunctively denied, in the minor, and the antecedents disjunctively denied, in the conclusion.
E.G. " If A is B, C is D, and if E is F, G is H;
but either C is not D, or G is not H; therefore
either A is not B, or E is not F."—" If a witness
be an honest one, he will not bear false testimony

---

instead of *disjunctively*, denied in the minor. This is,
however, a mere combination of *simple* conditional syllogisms, two or more being expressed together. It may consist either—1st, of one antecedent with several consequents;
or, 2ndly, of several antecedents with one consequent; or,
3rdly, of several antecedents with several consequents.
1st, If A is B, C is D; if A is B, E is F; if A is B, G is H;
but C is not D, E is not F, G is not H; therefore A is not
B. 2ndly, If A is B, C is D; if E is F, C is D; if G is H,
C is D; but C is not D; therefore A is not B, E is not F,
G is not H. 3rdly, If A is B, C is D; if E is F, G is H;
if I is K, L is M; but C is not D, G is not H, L is not M;
therefore A is not B, E is not F, I is not K. Should you,
in the first case, deny the consequents *disjunctively* instead
of *categorically*, you will not thereby make the argument a
dilemma; for if *all* the consequents be not true, the *one
antecedent* must fall to the ground. E. G. " If A is B, C
is D; if A is B, E is F; if A is B, G is H; but either C is
not D, E is not F, or G is not H; therefore A is not B.
But in the correct destructive dilemma there is always a
disjunctive conclusion.

E

designedly; and if he be a competent one, he will not do so undesignedly : but a witness who speaks false, does so either designedly or undesignedly ; therefore he is either not honest or not competent."

77. The dilemma may always be reduced into simple conditional syllogisms, by adding a categorical minor to each antecedent and consequent of the major premiss of the dilemma. On such a statement, it will be seen that an opponent could not deny *both* the minors, and that he must, therefore, admit *one* of the conclusions.

78. In a constructive dilemma, some one of the antecedents is assumed to be true ; and, in a destructive, some one of the consequents assumed to be false ; but *which*, is left undetermined.

REDUCTION OF HYPOTHETICAL SYLLOGISMS.

79. To reduce a hypothetical syllogism into a categorical form, you must view every conditional proposition as a universal affirmative, taking the antecedent for the subject, and the consequent for the predicate.

	Anteced.	*Conseq.*		*Subject.*		*Predicate.*
Bar-	If |A is B,|	|C is D;|		The case of A being B |	is	| the case of C being D; |
-ha-	But A is B; therefore			The present case is that of A being B; therefore		
-ra.	C is D.			The present case is that of C being D.		

	Anteced.	*Conseq.*		*Subject.*		*Predicate.*
Cam-	If |A is B,|	|C is not D;|		The case of A being B, |	is	| the case of C not being D; |
-es-	But C is D; therefore			The present case is not the case of C not being D; therefore		
-tres.	A is not B.			The present case is not the case of A being B.		

Camestres may, of course, be reduced to *Celarent.*
But even destructive conditionals may be stated in
Barbara, if you view them as constructive; which
is done by converting by negation the major premiss. (See No. 68, *Note.*) This process of reduction, however, is explained merely to show the
applicability of Aristotle's dictum to every form of
argument; since the rules for hypothetical syllogisms are a sufficient test of their validity.

ENTHYMEMES.

80. The Enthymeme is a syllogism, with one of
the premises omitted. This premiss is easily supplied by comparing the middle term with that term
of the conclusion which is expressed *only once.*
E. G.

"Isaiah was a prophet; therefore
He was inspired."

The middle term, of course, is that which does
not enter into the conclusion, viz. "Prophet."
—"Isaiah," or the minor term, is expressed *twice.*
"Inspired," the major term, *only once.* Compare,
therefore, the middle term with the major, thus supplying the major premiss; E. G.

" Every prophet is inspired;

Isaiah was a prophet; therefore

He was inspired."

If the minor premiss had been suppressed, the minor term "Isaiah" could have occurred *only once*. E. G.

" Every prophet is inspired; therefore

Isaiah was inspired."

You must, in that case, have taken the minor term "Isaiah" for comparison with the middle, thus supplying the minor premiss.*

81. By taking the two propositions of an enthymeme for an antecedent and consequent, you may form it into a conditional syllogism; E. G. "If Isaiah was a prophet, he was inspired."

OF THE SORITES.

82. A Sorites* is a brief form of connecting several syllogisms in the first figure. In a sorites, the predicate of the first proposition is made the

---

* This is the ordinary way of speaking and writing, and in this concise form we continually reason in our minds, ἐν θυμῷ. Hence the term Enthymeme.

† From σωρὸς, a pile; because the propositions are *piled*, as it were, one on another.

subject of the next, and so on, to any length, till finally the predicate of the last of the premises is predicated, in the conclusion, of the subject of the first.

A is B;	Religion improves the morals;
B is C;	What improves the morals is beneficial to the community;
C is D; therefore	What is beneficial to the community deserves encouragement; therefore
A is D;	Religion deserves encouragement.

83. In a sorites, there are as many middle terms as there are intermediate propositions between the first and last; the subject of each intermediate proposition being a middle term. A sorites may, therefore, be drawn out into as many separate syllogisms as there are intermediate propositions.

84. In drawing out a sorites into distinct* syllogisms, you must take for your major premiss the *first intermediate* proposition of the sorites, and

---

* By *distinct* and *separate* syllogisms, I mean those *in form*, with major, minor, and conclusion, into which the sorites may be expanded.

for your minor premiss, the *first* proposition of it;
then draw your conclusion. The major proposition of your next syllogism must be the *second intermediate proposition* of the sorites, and your
minor proposition must be the conclusion of your
preceding syllogism; thence draw your second
conclusion. Proceed thus till you have formed as
many distinct syllogisms as the sorites contains
intermediate propositions, and have arrived at the
same conclusion. The sorites gives you only the
first minor premiss, viz. in its first proposition.
All the other *minor* premises consist of the conclusions of your separate syllogisms. All your
major premises consist of the intermediate propositions of the sorites. E. G.

Intermediate Propositions.

" A is B, ⌈B is C, C is D, D is E,⌉ therefore
A is E." Here is a sorites with three intermediate
propositions, to be drawn out into three distinct
syllogisms.

Syll. 1.	*Syll.* 2.	*Syll.* 3.
B is C;	C is D;	D is E;
A is B; therefore	A is C; therefore	A is D; therefore
A is C.	A is D.	A is E.

85. In a sorites, the *first* proposition alone (except, of course, the conclusion) may be *particular;* because the first proposition is made the minor of the distinct syllogism (No. 84) and may be particular, according to rule, (either Dar*i*i, or Fer*i*o.) The intermediate propositions being all majors of the distinct syllogisms, must be universals. (Barbara, Celarent, Darii, Fer*i*o.)

86. The last premiss of the sorites (viz. the last intermediate proposition) is the only one that can be negative;"* because the last premiss alone never gives occasion to employ the conclusion of the distinct syllogism as the minor of a subsequent one. Should any other premiss of the sorites but the last be negative, it would lead to a negative conclusion, (No. 37, Rule 6,) and that conclusion, being made the minor of the following syllogism, would violate the first figure, which does not admit of a negative minor premiss. (Barbara, Celarent, Dar*i*i, Fer*i*o.)

87. A hypothetical sorites consists of a series of hypothetical syllogisms. In the constructive hy-

---

* Should a sorites *appear* to have a negative premiss before the last, the succeeding premiss will shew that the negative is, in reality, a part of one of the terms.

pothetical sorites, you proceed from the establishment of the first antecedent to the establishment
of the last consequent.   E. G.

If A is B, C is D;   If it is the duty of a parent to
take care of his children, he
should keep them, as much
as possible, from vice;

If C is D, E is F;   If he should keep them from
vice, he ought to teach them
what is virtuous;

If E is F, G. is H;   If he ought to teach them what
is virtuous, he is bound to
instruct them in religious
knowledge;

But A is B;   But it is the duty of a parent
therefore   to take care of his children;
therefore

G is H.   He is bound to instruct them
in religious knowledge.

In a destructive sorites, you go back from the denial of the last consequent, to the denial of the first
antecedent; "G is not H; therefore A is not B."

"If Romish councils speak the truth, popery
should be credited;

If popery should be credited, protestantism is
   fallacious;

If protestantism is fallacious, the Scriptures
   are not the rule of faith;

But the Scriptures are the rule of faith; therefore

Romish councils do not speak the truth."

OF INDUCTION.

88. Induction* is a kind of argument, which in-
fers, respecting a whole class, what has been ascer-
tained respecting one or more subdivisions of that
class; or the drawing a general conclusion from as
many particular instances as can be *brought in* to
bear on the point in question; as if, on perceiving
that the ox, sheep, deer, goat, and antelope, all ruminate, you should infer that *all horned animals*
ruminate. Inductive arguments, which are usually
stated as enthymemes,† (No. 80.) are, of course,
easily filled up, so as to become regular syllogisms.

---

* The term " Induction " is sometimes employed to designate the process of investigating and collecting facts;
which is not a process of argument, but a *preparation for it*.

† The example given by Dr. Aldrich is inconveniently
stated for reduction into a syllogistic form, a circumstance

EPICHIREMA.

89. One of the premises of a syllogism is occasionally confirmed by an incidental proposition, called a Prosyllogism. This proposition, with the premiss it is attached to, form an enthymeme. (No. 80.) The *incidental* proposition is the *expressed premiss* of the enthymeme, and the premiss it is attached to is the *conclusion.* E. G.

   " All sin is dangerous;

      Covetousness is sin; (for it is a transgression
         of the Law;) therefore

      It is dangerous."

---

which, perhaps, occasioned his error, (pointed out by Dr. Whately,) in directing the student to supply the minor, instead of the major, premiss of the enthymeme; " Hic et ille et iste magnes trahit ferrum ; ergo omnis." The real subject here is, "ferrum trahere," the real predicate, "proprium hujus et illius et istius magnetis." The term expressed *but once* will be the major, "proprium omnis," which must therefore be compared with the middle, (No. 80.) viz. "proprium hujus, et illius, et istius magnetis."

Middle Term.

| " What belongs to this, that, and the other magnet, | is

Major Term.

| what belongs to all; |

Minor Term.   *Middle*

| The power of attracting iron | is | what belongs to

Term.

this, that, and the other magnet; | therefore

Minor Term.   *Major Term.*

| The power of attracting iron | is | what belongs to all." |

The minor premiss is an enthymeme; "Covetousness is a transgression of the law; therefore it is sin." A syllogism with such a premiss is called an Epichirema. (ἐπιχειρέω, I undertake to prove.)

EQUIVALENTS.

90. Equivalent terms are allowable for brevity's sake, as the pronoun for the noun; equivalent propositions are also allowable, as the illative converse for the exposita; (No. 30 *et seq.*) and such equivalents as may be supplied by ranking species under genus, &c.

IRREGULAR SYLLOGISMS.

91. The premises of a valid syllogism may appear negative, contrary to Rule 5, No. 37. One of the premises should then be stated as an affirmative. (See *Note* to No. 33, " It is the same," &c.)

"No one is wise who is not virtuous;

No gamester is virtuous; therefore

No gamester is wise."

The real middle term in this syllogism is, " notvirtuous," and it is in *Celarent.*

" He who is not-virtuous is not wise;

A gamester is not-virtuous; therefore

He is not wise.'

92. From the variety of expression admissible in language, the logical order of subject and predicate is often inverted; and this will occasion the appearance of too many terms in the syllogism. All that is requisite, in such cases, is to restore the subject and predicate to their proper order. E.G.

"No irrational agent could produce a work which manifests design;

The universe is a work which manifests design; therefore

No irrational agent could have produced the universe."

Strictly considered, this syllogism has five terms, viz. 1. An irrational agent. 2. A being, able to produce a work which manifests design. 3. The universe. 4. A work which manifests design. 5. A being, able to produce the universe.

" | A work which manifests design | | could not
Middle Term. *Copula*

be produced by an irrational agent; |
and Major Term.

| The universe | is | a work which manifests
Minor Term. *Middle*

design; | therefore
Term.

| It | | could not be produced by an irrational agent."
Minor T. *Copula and Major Term.*

93. The above irregularity is sometimes accompanied with a transposition of the premises, as in the following syllogism, which appears to be in the second figure, and faulty, from an affirmative conclusion. (*Note* to No. 47.)

> "Every true patriot is disinterested;
> Few men are disinterested; therefore
> Few men are true patriots."

It is, in reality, *Barbara*, with a transposition of the premises, and of the terms of the major proposition; for you do not predicate of "few men," that they are "disinterested," but of "disinterested men," that they are "few."

> " Disinterested men are few;
> True patriots are disinterested men; therefore
> True patriots are few."

94. By the use of conversion and equipollent propositions, such irregularities as the following are easily reduced to form.

> "None but candid men are good reasoners;
> Few infidels are candid; therefore
> Few infidels are good reasoners."

The major premiss here is equipollent to " They who are not candid men are not good reasoners," which is the converse by negation of " All good reasoners are candid men." (No. 30.)   State your

major proposition in A accordingly.   The minor
premiss and the conclusion are equipollent to
" Most infidels are not candid ;" therefore " Most
infidels are not good reasoners."   This will be a
regular syllogism in *Camestres* or *Fakoro ;** or it
may be stated at once in *Celarent,* or *Ferio.*

"They who are not candid (or uncandid)

<u>*Copula*</u>
⌈are not⌉ good reasoners;

<u>*Copula*</u>
Most infidels ⌊are⌉ notcandid ; (or uncandid;)
therefore

<u>*Copula*</u>
Most infidels ⌊are not⌉ good reasoners."†

---

* I have said *Camestres* or Fakoro, and *Celarent* or
Ferio, because "most" cannot designate *absolute* universality, though the present case may be thought to amount
to a *moral* one. (See *Note* to No. 15, and Universality,
in the Index.)

† For the attainment of skill in syllogizing, as in every
other intellectual process, true it is, that "sapere est et
principium et fons."   Without good sense and some command of expression, it will often be very difficult for a student to state, *in form*, many arguments that are sufficiently
conclusive.   On the other hand, some proficiency in logic,
as an *art*, is essential to the ready performance of this
exercise, however simple it may appear.   Though good
sense and command of expression are indispensable, they
are not, of themselves, sufficient. A study, then, which
both tries the faculties of the *mind*, and calls into play the
resources of *phraseology*, is surely to be considered as
worthy of a place in the scheme of a liberal education.

EXERCISES.

Add the proper Symbols to the following Propositions.

1. All grief is mitigated by time. (No. 15.)

2. Some troubles happen to all. (No. 15.)

3. No deceit is justifiable. (No. 15.)

4. Reverence is due to God. (No. 19.)

5. Some virtuous men have been unfortunate.

6. A dissipated character is not estimable. (No. 19.)

7. Many ingenious men have not acquired a reputation. (No. 15.)

8. The rose soon fades. (No. 19.)

9. Alexander was the son of Philip. (No. 11, *note.*)

10. Herodotus is not to be implicitly believed.

11. Few men are acquainted with themselves. (No. 15, *note.*)

12. Sin is necessarily destructive of happiness. (No. 12, *note.*)

13. Every animal is either rational or irrational. (No. 13.)

14. There is no one free from faults. (No. 15.)

15. Rome was the mistress of the world.

16. "Thou art the man."

17. Reading improves the mind. (No. 19.)

18. The Chinese are an idolatrous people. (No. 11, *note.*)

19. Romulus and Remus were twins.

20. If a man be a diligent student, he will become learned. (No. 13.)

21. Every mistake that a man makes is not a sign of folly. (No. 15.)

22. All men have not great abilities.

23. None but classical scholars can fully appreciate the beauties of ancient literature. (No. 15.)

24. "None is lost but the son of perdition.'

State the Contraries and Contradictories of the following Propositions. (*No.* 27.)

25. No men are immortal.

26. No conscientious person is deserving of ridicule.

27. All falsehood is dangerous.

28. Every real Christian is charitable.

29. Dishonesty deserves to be punished.

30. Nothing past can be recalled.

31. All who know what is right are bound to practise it.

32. Not one of the enemy escaped.

How, in respect of quantity, is the contradictory of each of the above propositions related to the contrary ?

State the Subcontraries and Contradictories of the following Propositions.

33. Some evils are inseparable from a state of mortality.

34. Many apparent misfortunes are real blessings.

35. Several writers of merit have not been popular.

36. All do not admire the same things.— *Hor.*

37. Some men are eager for novelty.

38. Many critics are not candid judges.

39. Few can distinguish between what is really good and evil.—*Juv.*

40. All the hexameters of Virgil are not completed.

-----

41. No miser is contented.

What is the symbol of this proposition? (No. 17.) Is its simple converse true ? (No. 33, or 34.)

42. Some misfortunes are unavoidable.

Add the symbol. What is the contradictory ? Is it true or false ? (Nos. 26, 27, 28.) What is the

simple converse of the contradictory? Is it true
or false? What is the contradictory of the simple
converse? How may this be changed into the
exposita? (No. 30.)

43. No good man is a liar.

Add the symbol. What is the simple converse?
Is it true? (No. 33.) What is the subalternate
of the simple converse? (Nos. 24, 27.) How
might the exposita be changed into this? (No. 33.)

44. All earthly things are perishable.

Add the symbol. What is the subalternate?
Is it true? (No. 28.). What is the simple converse of the subalternate? Is it true? How
might the exposita be changed into it? No. 30.)

EXERCISES ON SYLLOGISM, ETC.

45. Swearing is forbidden by our Saviour;
swearing is practised in our Courts of Justice;
therefore something practised in our Courts of
Justice is forbidden by our Saviour.

Is this fallacious? See the Church Articles;
also (Nos. 19 and 37, Rule 3.)

46. Hypocrisy is injurious to the interests of
religion; ill-directed zeal is often taken for hypocrisy; therefore it is injurious to the interests of
religion.

Is the conclusion true? Does it follow? Why? (No. 37, Rule 1.)

47. Covetousness is idolatry; to worship graven images is idolatry; therefore it is covetousness. (No. 37, Rule 3.)

48. No bribery is defensible; bribery is not idleness; therefore idleness is not defensible. (No. 37, Rule 5.)

Is the conclusion true? Does it follow? Why?

49. Mathematical study improves the reasoning powers; the study of logic is not mathematical study; therefore it does not improve the reasoning powers. (No. 37, Rule 4.)

50. Whatever is sinful is productive of sorrow; fraud and revenge are sinful, and poverty deprives us of many comforts; therefore fraud, revenge, and poverty are all productive of sorrow. (No. 37, Rule 2.)

51. Some sins are not malicious; calumny is a sin; therefore it is malicious. (No. 37, Rule 6, and 3.)

52. All luxury is sinful; all luxury is agreeable to the bodily sense; therefore whatever is agreeable to the bodily sense is sinful. (No. 37, Rule 4.)

53. No religious man is factious; St. Paul was a religious man; therefore he was not factious.

What mood and figure? (Nos. 41, 45.)

54. Some vicious pastimes are permitted by law; every vicious pastime is disgraceful to a Christian; therefore something disgraceful to a Christian is permitted by law.

What mood and figure? How reducible? Could you say, "Every thing disgraceful to a Christian is permitted by law?" Why? (No. 37. Rule 4.)

55. No men are free from sin; every one free from sin is the servant of God; therefore some servants of God are not men.

What mood and figure, and how reducible?

56. Whoever winneth souls is wise; all who preach the Gospel faithfully win souls; therefore some who preach the Gospel faithfully are wise.

Has this mood any name? What conclusion might you draw? (No. 44, *note*.)

57. No wicked people enjoy peace of mind; all who have gained riches dishonestly are wicked people; therefore some who have gained riches dishonestly do not enjoy peace of mind.

Is this valid? What is the name of the mood? State the *subalternans* of the conclusion. (No. 44, *note*, and No. 24.)

58. If Roman history is credible, the Carthaginians were a treacherous people; Roman history is credible; therefore the Carthaginians were a treacherous people. (No. 67.)

59. St. Matthew's Gospel is allowed to have been first written either in Greek or Hebrew; Erasmus thought it was not first written in Hebrew; therefore he thought it was first written in Greek. (No. 71.)

60. All parts of Scripture are written for our learning; some dreadful narratives are parts of Scripture; therefore some dreadful narratives are written for our learning.

What mood and figure?

61. Every candid man acknowledges merit in a rival; every learned man does not acknowledge merit in a rival; therefore every learned man is not candid.

What are the quantity and quality of the minor premiss and the conclusion? (No. 15.) What mood and figure? Reduce the syllogism.

62. All earthly projects are liable to disappointment; nothing liable to disappointment should engage our chief concern; therefore something that should engage our chief concern is not an earthly project.

Might you substitute the *subalternans* of the conclusion ? In what mood and figure would the syllogism then be ?

63. Immoral companions should be avoided; some immoral companions are intelligent; therefore some intelligent persons should be avoided. (No. 19.) State the mood, figure, and mode of reduction.

64. If the world were good, laws would be useless; but laws are not useless; therefore the world is not good. (No. 67, Rule 2.)

65. If the world were good, laws would be useless; but the world is not good; therefore laws are not useless.

Is this conclusive ? Why ? (No. 68.)

66. Make a disjunctive syllogism from 2 *Samuel*, xxiv, 13.

67. What sort of proposition is it in *Luke* xvi, 30 ? Can you make of it a valid syllogism ? Which is the *Consequentia* ? (No. 65.)

68. If I am blest with opulence, I have reason to be thankful; but I am not blest with opulence; therefore I have no reason to be thankful. (No. 68.)

69. If I am blest with opulence, I have reason

to be thankful; but I have reason to be thankful; therefore I am blest with opulence.

70. Every vicious amusement is unbecoming a wise man; no philosophical pursuits are unbecoming a wise man; therefore some philosophical pursuits are not vicious amusements.

In what figure is this syllogism? The mood?

71. If a proposition be a particular affirmative, shew to what sorts of propositions it cannot belong. Prove this by a syllogism. (No. 71.)

72. The Helvetii, if they went through the country of the Sequani, were sure to meet with various difficulties; and if they went through the Roman province, they were exposed to the danger of opposition from Cæsar; but they were obliged to go one way or the other; therefore they were either sure of meeting with various difficulties, or exposed to the danger of opposition from Cæsar.— *De Bello Gallico, lib.* i. 6.

What sort of argument is this? (No. 75.) Reduce it into simple syllogisms. (No. 77.)

73. This man has been proved treacherous; therefore he is not to be trusted.

What sort of argument? supply the premiss. (No. 80.)

74. If pain is violent, it should be borne with patience, because it will be of short continuance; and if it be slight, it should be borne with patience, because it is only a small evil; but pain must be either violent or slight; therefore it should be borne with patience.

What sort of argument? (No. 74.) What do you call the two incidental propositions in the major premiss? (No. 89.)

75. No woman of great mind would submit to the indignity of being led in triumph; therefore Cleopatra would not.

What sort of argument? Supply the premiss.

76. Our heavenly Father is merciful; therefore we should be merciful.*

77. Alexander was buried; he who is buried becomes dust; what becomes dust is earth; earth is probably made loam; what is probably made loam might probably stop a beer-barrel; therefore Alexander might probably stop a beer-barrel. See *Hamlet, Act* V, *Scene* 1.

---

* In supplying the deficient premiss, the strict form of syllogism will be better preserved, if we state the above propositions thus: "To be merciful is a quality of our heavenly Father; therefore it should be ours." (No. 80.)

What sort of argument? Into how many distinct syllogisms may it be expanded, and why? State it in this form. (Nos. 82, 83, and 84.).

78. None but pious men are fit for the priesthood; some ignorant men are pious; therefore some ignorant men are fit for the priesthood.

Is this valid? Why? (No. 15, and No. 37, Rule 3.)

79. None but the truly penitent are pardoned; the malefactor mentioned by St. Luke (ch. xxiii.) was truly penitent; therefore he was pardoned.

Is this conclusion true? Does it follow from the premises? What major proposition does the conclusion require?

80. If man is responsible for his actions, he ought to live circumspectly; if he ought to live circumspectly, he should consider what is his duty; if he should consider what is his duty, it concerns him to seek the will of God; if it concerns him to seek the will of God, he ought to study the holy Scriptures; but man is responsible for his actions; therefore it is incumbent on him to study the holy Scriptures.

What sort of argument? to which division does

it belong, and why ? (No. 87.) How could it be changed, so as to fall under the other division ? Would the proposition, in that case, be true ?

81. All great poets are men of genius; Cicero was a man of genius; therefore he was a great poet. (No. 37, Rule 3.)

82. Opulence is seen, in such a multitude of instances, to harden the heart and to engross the soul, that we might conclude, even without the authority of Scripture, that the rich enter with difficulty into the kingdom of Heaven.

What sort of argument ? (No. 88.)

83. Whatever tends to withdraw the mind from pursuits of a low nature deserves to be promoted; classical learning does this, since it gives us a taste for intellectual enjoyments; therefore it deserves to be promoted.

What name is given to such a syllogism as this ? Which is the prosyllogism ? Which premiss is of itself an enthymeme ? (No. 89.)

84. A negro is a fellow-creature; therefore he who injures a negro injures a fellow-creature.*

---

* This kind of argument, though not formal, is so obviously valid, that it were a waste of time to expand it into

85. No virtuous man is malevolent; all detractors are malevolent; therefore some detractors are not virtuous.

86. He is brave who conquers his passions: he who resists temptation conquers his passions; therefore he who resists temptation is brave.

87. All the ships that sailed to Troy, contained, probably, 100,000 men; the ship of Nireus was one of these; (Il. B. 671.) therefore it probably contained 100,000 men. (No. 37, Rule 3. See FALLACIÆ, in the Index.)

88. Somebody must obtain the high prize in every lottery; each individual who holds a ticket is somebody; therefore each individual who holds a ticket must obtain the high prize. (No. 37, Rule 3.)

---

syllogisms. It will be found to rest upon the general principle, that whatever stands in any relation to an individual or species, bears the same relation to a part of any class or predicable which comprehends that individual or species. E. G. "What stands in any relation to the species 'Negro,' bears the same relation to the predicable, 'Fellow-creature,' which comprehends the species 'Negro;' he who injures a 'Negro,' stands in a relation to the species 'Negro,' therefore he who injures a 'Negro,' bears the same relation to the predicable, 'Fellow-creature,' which comprehends the species 'Negro.'"

89. Sticks are easily broken; fagots are sticks; therefore fagots are easily broken. (No. 37, Rule 3.) See FALLACIÆ, in the Index.

90. Books are a source both of instruction and pleasure; the Iliad and Odyssey are books; therefore they are a source both of instruction an pleasure. (No. 19, No. 37, Rule 3.)

INDEX AND VOCABULARY.

ABSOLUTE *Noun*, or *Term*, See TERM.

ABSTRACT *Noun*, or *Term*, See Term.

ABSTRACTION, the process by which we draw off, in thought, from a notion, any circumstances we do not purpose to consider. By this process generalization is performed.

ACCIDENT, a predicable *contingently* joined to the essence of the species, and which may, therefore, be absent or present, the essence of the species remaining the same; as, "A man *walking*," "A man *born at Paris*." The former is called a *separable* accident, because it may be separated from the individual; the latter is plainly *inseparable*. Accident is predicated in *Quale*. See SPECIES.

ACCIDENTAL DEFINITION, See DEFINITION.

ANALOGOUS *Words* or *Terms*, See WORDS.

ANTECEDENT, No. 65.

APPREHENSION, *Simple*, one of the three operations of the mind concerned in argument. The notion of any object in the mind. It is either *Incomplex* or *Complex*. See OPERATIONS.

APPREHENSION, *Simple Incomplex*, the notion of one object, as, "A pen," or of several objects confusedly and without any relation, as, "Pens."

APPREHENSION, *Simple Complex,* the notion of two or more objects between which there is some relation, as, " A pen in the hand."

ARGUMENT, an act of reasoning expressed in language; popularly speaking, the means by which some point is proved.

CANONS *of Syllogisms,* No. 36.

CATEGOREMATIC *Word,* or CATEGOREM, from κατηγορέω, I predicate, a word that may be employed by itself as a term. Such words are also called *Simple terms.*

CATEGORIES *of Aristotle,* or *Ten Predicaments.* General heads, to one or more of which every term may be referred, viz. οὐσία, πόσον, ποῖον, πρόστι, ποιεῖν, πάσχειν, ποῦ, πότε, κεῖσθαι, ἔχειν. Substance, quantity, quality, relation, action, passion, (or suffering,) place, time, situation, possession, (or covering.)

CAUSE, *Divisions of,* 1st. *Efficient, (à quâ,)* either *Principal,* as the *shoemaker, by whom* the shoe is made; or *Instrumental,* as the *awl, knife,* &c. *with which* the shoe is made. 2nd. *Material, (ex quâ,)* either *Proximate,* as the *leather of which* the shoe is made; or *Remote,* as the *skin of which* the leather is made. 3rd, *Formal, (per quam,)* either *Proximate,* as the *shape* or *fashion* of the *shoe;* (because the material so shaped becomes a shoe;) or *Remote,* as the *natural form* of the *leather* (viz. that which is essential to its being leather) is the more remote form of the shoe. 4th. *Final; (propter quam;)* denoting the *end for which* a thing is made or done; either *Proximate,* as the proximate end for which a shoe is made, is the *protection of the foot;* or *Remote,* as its more remote end is the comfort and health of the body.

dental; and essential definition is further divided into *physical* and *logical,* (or *metaphysical.*)

DEFINITION, *Essential,* one which assigns the constituent parts of the essence or nature; either the *real* parts of the essence, which are *actually separable,* as if, in defining " Plant," you should enumerate the leaves, stalks, roots, &c. which is a *physical* definition; or the *ideal* parts, which are *separable only in the mind,* as when a plant is defined to be " an organized being, destitute of sensation," which is a *logical* or *metaphysical* definition. N.B. A *logical* definition must always consist of the *genus* and *differentia.*

DEFINITION, *Accidental,* commonly called a *Description;* that definition of a thing which is given by assigning to it the circumstances *belonging* to its essence; viz. Properties and Accidents; (causes, effects, &c.) E. G. " Barometer," " A machine for measuring the weight of the atmosphere." " Balloon," " A silken ball, filled with gas, which causes it to rise into the air." " Lion," " The fiercest and most noble of quadrupeds," &c.

DEFINITION, *three principal Rules for.* 1st. A definition must be adequate, *i.e.* neither too narrow nor too extensive. If it be too narrow, you explain *a part* instead of *a whole;* if too extensive, *a whole* instead of *a part.* 2nd. It must be of itself clearer (*i.e.* consist of ideas less complex) than the thing defined. 3rd. It must be couched in just a sufficient number of proper words. *Proper* is here used in opposition to *metaphorical,* which class of words is excluded on account of their vague and *indefinite* nature. H

VIDUAL.) In the former, you may predicate the divided whole of every dividing member. Thus, "Weapon" may be predicated of "Sword," "Pike," "Gun." This cannot happen in the case of physical division. "Gun" cannot be predicated of "the Lock," "the Stock," or "the Barrel."

DIVISION, *Rules for logical*, are *three*. 1st, Each of the parts, or any, short of all, must contain less (*i. e.* have a narrower signification) than the thing divided. "Weapon" could not be a division of the term "Sword." 2nd. All the parts together must be exactly equal to the thing divided. In dividing the term "Weapon," into "Sword," "Pike," "Gun," &c. we must not omit any thing of which "Weapon," can be predicated, nor introduce any thing of which it cannot. 3rd. The parts or members must be *opposed;* *i. e.* must not be contained in one another. "Book" must not be divided into "Quarto," "French," for a French book may be a quarto, and a quarto, French. N.B. You must always keep in mind the *Principle of Division*, with which you set out; E.G. whether you begin to divide books according to their *size, language, matter*, &c.

ENTHYMEME, Nos. 80, 81.

EPICHIREMA, No. 89.

EQUIVALENTS, No. 90.

ESSENCE, the nature of any being, whether actually existing or not; "Snow" has an *essence* in summer; in winter, it has existence also.

EXPOSITA, *what*, No. 30.

EXTREMES, No. 7, and *note*, and No. 37, *note*.

FALLACY, an argument, or apparent argument, professing to decide the matter at issue, while it really does not.

FALLACIA ÆQUIVOCATIONIS, arising from the use of an equivocal word; E. G. "The dog is an animal; Sirius is the dog; therefore Sirius is an animal." See No. 37, Rule 3rd.

FALLACIA AMPHIBOLIÆ, or *doubtful Construction;* E. G. "Quod tangitur à Socrate illud sentit; columna tangitur à Socrate; ergo columna sentit." In the major proposition, "sentit" means "he, *i. e.* Socrates, feels." In the conclusion, the same word means "feels Socrates." See No. 37, Rule 1st.

FALLACIA COMPOSITIONIS, when what is proposed in a *divided* sense is afterwards taken *collectively;* E. G. "Two and three are even and odd; five is two and three; therefore five is even and odd." See No. 37, Rule 3rd.

FALLACIA DIVISIONIS, when what is proposed in a *collective,* is afterwards taken in a *divided* sense; E. G. "The planets are seven; Mercury and Venus are planets; therefore Mercury and Venus are seven." · See No. 37, Rule 3rd.

FALLACIA FIGURÆ DICTIONIS, when, from any similitude between two words, what is granted of one is, by a forced application, predicated of another; as, "Projectors are not fit to be trusted, therefore he who has formed a project is not· fit to be trusted" —*See Dr. Whately's Logic, ch.* iii. § 8.

FALLACIA ACCIDENTIS, when what is accidental is confounded with what is essential; E. G. "What you bought you have eaten; raw meat is what you bought; therefore raw meat is what you have eaten." In the major proposition, "What you bought" means *as regards its Essence;* in the minor, *as regards its Accidents.* See No. 37, Rule 3rd.

FALLACIA A DICTO SECUNDUM QUID AD DICTUM SIMPLICITER, when a Term is at one time used in a limited, at another, in an unlimited sense, as, "The Ethiopian is *white as to his teeth;* therefore he is *white.*" See No. 37, Rule 1st.

FALLACIA IGNORATIONIS ELENCHI, an argument that indicates ignorance of the point in dispute; an irrelevant conclusion; as.if any one, to shew the inutility of the art of Logic, should prove that men unacquainted with it have reasoned well.

FALLACIA A NON CAUSA PRO CAUSA, which is divided into *Fallacia à non verâ pro verâ,* and *Fallacia à non tali pro tali.* E.G. "A comet has appeared, therefore there will be war."—" What intoxicates should be prohibited, and wine intoxicates." The abuse of it does. In replying, you should deny the false cause, or assign the true one.

FALLACIA CONSEQUENTIS, when that is inferred which does not logically follow; as, "He is an animal; therefore he is a man."

FALLACIA PETITIONIS PRINCIPII, (*begging the Question,*) when that is assumed for granted, which ought to have been proved; as when a thing is proved *by itself,* (called *Petitio statim,*) "He is a man, therefore he is a man;" or *by a Synonym,* as, "A sabre is sharp, therefore a cymetar is;" or *by any thing equally unknown,* as, "Paradise was in Armenia, therefore Gihon is an Asiatic river;" or *by any thing more unknown,* as, "This square is twice the size of this triangle, because equal to this circle;" or *by discoursing in a circle*, i. e. when the disputant tries to prove reciprocally conclusion from premises, and premises from conclusion ; as, " Fire is hot, therefore it burns ;" and afterwards, " Fire burns, therefore it is hot."

FALLACIA PLURIUM INTERROGATIONUM, when two or more questions, requiring each a separate answer, are proposed as one; so that if *one* answer be given, it must be inapplicable to *one* of the particulars asked; as, " Was Pisistratus the usurper and scourge of Athens?" The answer " No" would be false of the former particular, and " Yes" would be false of the latter. This fallacy is overthrown by giving to each particular a separate reply.

FALSE, *strictly*, denotes the quality of a proposition which states a thing *not as it is.*

FIGURES, Nos. 41 and 48.

GENERALIZATION, the abstracting or drawing off, in thought, the points of dissimilitude between several objects which resemble each other in some part of their nature, and the assigning to them one *common name* expressive of the particulars in which they all agree. Thus, " Pigeon," " Wren," " Eagle," " Cassowary," differ in *shape, plumage, size,* &c. but agree in being all *feathered creatures.* They come, therefore, under the general head of " Fowl," or " Bird."

GENERIC DIFFERENCE, See DIFFERENCE.

GENERIC PROPERTY, See PROPERTY.

GENUS, a Predicable, expressing the common or material part of the species of which it is affirmed. " Animal" is the genus of " Man." It is said to be predicated *in Quid.* See SPECIES.

PROPERTY, a Predicable expressing something necessarily joined to the essence of the whole species; whatever may be considered as the accompaniment or result of the *differentia.* "Risibility" is the property of "Man." Property is predicated in *Quale.* See SPECIES.

PROPERTY, *threefold division of.*—1st, Universal and peculiar; as, the *faculty of laughter* or *of speech*, to *man.* 2nd, Universal, but not peculiar; as, *the being a biped*, to *man. Every man* is a *biped*, but fowls are bipeds too. 3rd, Peculiar, but not universal, as, *the being a philosopher*, to *man.* Man *alone* can be a philosopher, but *every* man *is not* one. This third division, however, is more truly an *accident.*

PROPERTY, *Generic*, the property of a subaltern genus, and which may be predicated of all the subordinate species comprehended in that genus. "Voluntary motion" is the generic property of "Animal."

PROPERTY, *Specific*, the property of an *infima species*, and which may be predicated of all the individuals contained under it. "Risibility" is the specific property of "Man."

PROPOSITIO DE INESSE, *what*, No. 11, *Note.*

PROPOSITION, an act of judgment expressed in language, See No. 6.

PROPOSITION, *Affirmative*, Nos. 11 and 14.

PROPOSITION, *Categorical*, (*pure* and *modal*,) Nos. 11 and 12.

PROPOSITION, *Hypothetical*, (*conditional* and *disjunctive*,) Nos. 11 and 13.

PROPOSITION, *Indefinite*, No. 11, *Note.* No. 19.

Species subaltern, the same as subaltern genus ; i.e. one that is a genus, if viewed with reference to the species into which it is 'divisible. "Bird" is a *subaltern species,* being a *species* of *animal,* and the *genus* of *nightingale.*

Specific Difference, See Difference.

Specific Property, See Property.

Subaltern Propositions, See Propositions.

Subalternans, No. 24.

Subalternate, No. 24.

Subcontrary Propositions, See Propositions.

Subject, No. 6.

Substance *of a Proposition,* No. 11.

Syllogism, No. 2, No. 35.

Syllogisms,*Division of,* viz.Categorical,into Pure and Modal; Hypothetical, into Conditional and Disjunctive. No. 5.

Syllogisms, *Irregular,* Nos. 91, 92, 93, and 94.

Syllogisms, *Rules for ascertaining the validity of,* No. 37.

Symbols of *Quantity* and *Quality,* No. 17, No. 45.

Syncategorematic Word, or Syncategorem, (συγκατηγορέω, I predicate together with,) a word that can form only part of a term. Such are the particles of a language, and substantives in an oblique case. Adjectives and participles are generally accounted *Syncategorems.*

Term, an act of apprehension expressed in language. Also, the subject or predicate of a Proposition, No. 7.

Term, *Absolute,* one that is considered by itself, and conveys no idea of relation to any thing of which it is a part, or to any other part distinguished from it.

Term, *Abstract*, denotes the quality of a being, without regard to the subject in which it is ; as, " Justice," " Height," " Wisdom."   Abstract terms are nouns substantive.

Term, *Common*, such as stands for several individuals, which are called its *Significates* ; as "Man," "City." Such terms, and such only, can be affirmatively predicated of several others, and they are therefore called *Predicables*.

Terms, *Compatible* or *Consistent*, express two views which *can* be taken of the same object, at the same time, as, " White and Hard."

Term, *Complex*.   The same as Proposition.

Term, *Concrete*, denotes the quality of a being, and either expresses, or must be referred to, some subject in which it is; as,"Fool," "Foolish," "High," "Wise." Concrete Terms are usually, but not always, nouns adjective.

Terms, *Contradictory Opposition of*, when they differ only in respectively wanting and having the particle " not," or its equivalent.   *One or other* of such terms is applicable to *every* object.

Terms, *Contrary*, come both under some one class, but are the *most different* of all that belong to that class ; as, " Wise" and " Foolish," both coming under the class of mental qualities. There are some objects to which neither of such terms is applicable ; a Stone, for instance, is neither wise nor foolish.

Term, *Definite*, *(finitum,)* one which marks out an object or class of beings; as, " Cæsar," " Corporeal." *Positive* Terms are called *definite*.

TERM, *Indefinite, (infinitum,)* one which does not mark out, but only *exclude* an object, as, "Not-Cæsar," " Incorporeal." *Privative* and *negative* Terms are called *indefinite.*

TERM, *Negative*, denotes that the positive view *could not* be taken of the object; it affirms the absence of a thing from some subject in which it *could not* be present; as, " A dumb statue ;" (you could not say, " A speaking one.") " A lifeless corpse ;" (you could not say, " A living one.") N. B. The same term may be negative, positive, or privative, as it is viewed with relation to contrary ideas. Thus " Immortal" is privative or negative, viewed with relation to *Death,* and positive, viewed with relation to *Life.*

TERMS, *Opposite*, express two views which cannot be taken of one single object at the same time; as, " White and Black."

TERM, *Positive*, denotes a certain view of an object, as being actually taken of it; as, " Speech," " A man speaking."

TERM, *Privative*, denotes that the positive view *might* conceivably be taken of the object, but *is not;* " Dumbness," " A man silent ;" (you might say, "A man speaking.") "An unburied corpse ;" (you might say, ' A buried one.")

TERM, *Relative*, that which expresses an object viewed in relation to the whole, or to another part of a more complex object of thought, as " Half" and "Whole," " Master" and " Servant." Such nouns are called *Correlative* to each other; nor can one of them be mentioned, without a notion of the other being raised in the mind.

TERM, *Simple.* The same as CATEGOREMATIC WORD.

TERM, *Singular,* such as stands for one individual, as " Socrates," " London," " This man," " That city." Such terms cannot be predicated affirmatively of any thing but themselves.

UNDISTRIBUTED MIDDLE, No. 37, Rule 3.

UNIVERSALITY *of a Proposition.* A Proposition is *metaphysically* or *mathematically* universal, when the predicate belongs, without any exception, to every particular contained under the universal subject; as, " All circles have a centre and circumference." It is *physically* universal, when it always agrees, unless in the case of some unnatural exceptions; as, " All men are rational." It is *morally* universal, when it agrees in most instances, but not necessarily, or in the course of nature; as, " All the Cretans are liars."

WORDS, any combination of, making one complex apprehension, is, in logic, a *simple word;* as, " The-hope-of-reward is the-solace-of-labour." Every Proposition consists of three simple Words, viz. subject, copula, and predicate.

WORDS, *Various divisions of the manner of employing;* whence a word is called *Univocal, Equivocal, Analogous, of the first Intention, or of the second Intention.*

WORDS, *Univocal,* such as are confined to one meaning, and signify but one sort of idea; E.G. " Book," " Lance," " Tomb."

WORDS, *Equivocal,* such as signify two or more ideas; E. G. " Light," " Moor," " Pen," " Post."

WORDS, *Analogous,* such as signify two or more things that have no resemblance *in themselves,* but stand in a similar relation each to its respective object; E.G. "Hand," "Foot," "Sweet." As the *human hand points to* any object to which we would direct the attention, so does the *hand of a clock point to* the hour. As the *foot of an animal* is *the lowest part of it,* so is the *foot of a mountain* with relation to the mountain, &c.

WORDS, *of the first Intention,* such as are used in their vague and common acceptation; thus "Needle" signifies, in popular language, the *little steel instrument used in sewing.*

WORDS, *of the second Intention,* those to which a more precise and limited meaning is given, proper to some particular art, science, or system; thus "Needle" means, in the language of navigation, the *little steel bar in the mariner's compass.*

APPENDIX.

ON ACADEMICAL DISPUTATION.

THE Respondent, in a Disputation, being always supposed to maintain a true proposition, the argument of the Opponent, whose province it is to support the contradictory, must be presumed to be founded on some fallacy.

If the respondent, upon trying his opponent's objection in the form of a categorical syllogism, should find that it offends against any one of the six rules in No. 37, by pointing out such a violation, he overthrows the opponent's argument.

Should the objection be hypothetical, the respondent must examine the connexion between antecedent and consequent, (No.66,) and whether the

I

two rules at No. 67 have been observed. The detection also of any violation of the rules for drawing a conclusion from disjunctive propositions (Nos. 70, 71,) will destroy a fallacy so supported.

Fallacies that consist in a violation of the express rules of logic are more palpable than those which depend on the ambiguity of the middle term; by an ingenious application of which to the terms of the question, (No. 37, Rule 1,) fallacies are very generally introduced.

Most frequently, therefore, the first business of the respondent is to examine the middle term of his opponent's argument; and ascertain whether, in his comparison of it with the terms of his conclusion, he has used it in exactly the same sense in both instances. The first and second intention of words, their being employed sometimes in a literal, and sometimes in a metaphorical, sense, with other considerations arising from the various meanings attached to the same, or similar, terms, afford a wide scope for the exercise of fallacy, and call for acuteness, both natural and acquired, to detect it, if skilfully concealed.

The opponent has the choice of many points of

attack; for if he prove that the proposition advanced by the respondent appears at all inconsistent with any part of the system he is defending, or at variance with any received principle of truth, &c. or expressed in terms of too extensive a latitude,—by driving the respondent to explain such a difficulty, he has fairly executed his task.

The Cambridge argument now practised by the opponent at a public disputation in the schools, generally consists of three constructive conditional syllogisms (No. 67.)   The consequent (No. 65) in the first syllogism, is always, " Cadit quæstio."   If the respondent should deny the consequence, (or conclusion,) then the consequent of the second syllogism will be, " Valet consequentia ;" on the contrary, if he should deny the minor, (No. 64,) the consequent of the second syllogism will be, " Valet minor."   If the respondent should deny the consequence of the second syllogism, the consequent of the third will be, " Valent consequentia et argumentum ;" if he should deny the minor of the second, the consequent of the third will be, "Valent minor et argumentum."

Whichever proposition the respondent has denied, (whether it be the minor or consequence,) the opponent, in his next syllogism, affirms to be valid; taking for the consequent of his major proposition, "Valet minor," or "Valet consequentia," as the case may be.

Should the argument consist of only two syllogisms, the former will have for its consequent "Cadit quæstio," and the latter, either "Valent consequentia et argumentum," or "Valent minor et argumentum," according to the previous denial of the respondent. Should it consist of more than three, all, except the last, will have their consequent in the same manner as the second; either "Valet consequentia," or "Valet minor." The consequent of the concluding syllogism is always, "Valent consequentia et argumentum," or, "Valent minor et argumentum." It is not, however, advisable to use more than three syllogisms in constructing an argument for a disputation.

It is the duty of the respondent, at the close of each syllogism, either to concede or deny the minor proposition, as circumstances may require. If it be evidently true, he must, of course, concede it, but deny the consequence; viz. that its truth invalidates the question he is maintaining; "Concedo minorem, et nego consequentiam." If the minor be false, or doubtful, he denies it, ("Nego minorem,") and the opponent, on the other hand, must endeavour to establish it by some unquestionable medium of proof.

The following examples, exhibiting arguments of three, four, and two syllogisms, and shewing the mode of proceeding, as the minor or consequence may be denied in different places, will facilitate the application of the above remarks. The *Form* of the argument being at present the point for consideration, unmeaning symbols have been substituted for terms.

An Argument of three syllogisms, with the minor of the first denied.

OPPONENS.

MAJOR PROPOS.
Antecedent.   *Consequent.*
. 1. Si | A sit B, | ·| cadit quæstio ; |

MINOR PROPOS.
Sed A est B ;

· CONSEQUENTIA.
Ergo cadit quæstio.

RESPONDENS.

Nego minorem.

Pergit Dominus OPPONENS *ad syllogismum secundum.*

  2. Si C sit D, valet minor ;
    Sed C est D ;
    Ergo valet minor.

RESPONDENS.

Concedo minorem, et nego consequentiam.

Pergit OPPONENS *ad syllogismum tertium.*

  3. Si E sit F,valent consequentia et argumentum;
    Sed E est F ;
    Ergo valent consequentia et argumentum.

*An Argument of three syllogisms, with the minor
of the second denied.*

OPPONENS.

  1. Si A sit B, cadit quæstio ;
    Sed A est B ;
    Ergo cadit quæstio.

RESPONDENS.

Concedo minorem, et nego consequentiam.

OPPONENS *pergit ad syllogismum secundum.*

  2. Si C sit D, valet consequentia ;
    Sed C est D ;
    Ergo valet consequentia.

RESPONDENS.

Nego minorem.

Opponens *pergit ad syllogismum tertium.*

3. Si E sit F, valent minor et argumentum ;
   Sed E est F ;
   Ergo valent minor et argumentum.

*An Argument of four syllogisms, with the minor
of the second denied.*

Opponens.

1. Si A sit B, cadit quæstio;
   Sed A est B ;
   Ergo cadit quæstio.

Respondens.

Concedo minorem, et nego consequentiam.

Pergit Opponens.

2. Si C sit D, valet consequentia;
   Sed C est D ;
   Ergo valet consequentia.

Respondens.

Nego minorem.

Pergit Opponens.

3. Si E sit F, valet minor;
   Sed E est F ;
   Ergo valet minor.

Respondens.

Concedo minorem, et nego consequentiam.

Pergit Opponens.

4. Si G sit H, valent consequentia et argumentum ;
   Sed G est H ;
   Ergo valent consequentia et argumentum.

N. B. If the minor of the third syllogism had been denied, the consequent and conclusion of this last syllogism would have been, " Valent minor et argumentum."

An Argument of two syllogisms, with the minor of the first denied.

OPPONENS.

1. Si A sit B, cadit quæstio;
   Sed A est B ;
   Ergo cadit quæstio.

RESPONDENS.

Nego minorem.

Pergit OPPONENS.

2. Si C sit D, valent minor et argumentum ;
   Sed C est D ;
   Ergo valent minor et argumentum.

Should the minor of a concluding syllogism be false, the respondent does not say, "Nego minorem," but proceeds at once to his reply.

The antecedent, as may be seen in the preceding examples, is first enunciated in the subjunctive, or, at least, conditionally; then affirmed, in the minor premiss, in the indicative mood, and the consequent accordingly established.

It may happen, that the three conditional syllogisms admit of being reduced to the form of a single categorical syllogism; to the major, minor, and conclusion of which they severally correspond. But even in instances of this kind, it is not necessary that the three conditional syllogisms should be placed in the same order as the three propositions of the categorical syllogism, if the opponent thinks that, by a different arrangement, his sophism will be the better concealed.

The three conditional syllogisms of an opponent's argument, when they do not correspond with the three propositions of a categorical syllogism, would require, in order to be stated in form, to be expanded into two or more categorical syllogisms.

In responding to an opponent, it is by no means necessary to unfold in one's mind the objections he has adduced into as many strict categorical syllogisms as will lead to his conclusion; for this would often be a trifling and tedious process to the respondent; though it is highly desirable to possess the skill that would enable him, if required, to go through it.

Should the respondent, from the subtlety of his opponent's sophism, or any other cause, experience great difficulty in discovering the pith of the objection, the Moderator usually assists him, by restating the opponent's argument in a more lucid and intelligible form; and sometimes directing his attention to the quarter in which the fallacy is hidden.

It has been already stated to be the opponent's province, should the respondent deny the minor of his syllogism, to confirm it by some medium of proof. This, in the Divinity School, is generally done by an appeal to texts of Scripture; which, it may be observed, are commonly cited without being called for by the respondent, as they often afford ground for critical animadversion on the part of the professor, and opportunity for a further trial of the skill and knowledge of the disputants.

It is usual for the professor to call on the respondent for an interpretation into Latin of the more abstruse and difficult texts of the New Testament, that may happen to be quoted by the opponent. For citations from the Old Testament, the Vulgate is employed.*

When the respondent has replied to the opponent's objection, the moderator occasionally demands

---

* A copy of the Greek New Testament, and of the Vulgate version of the Old, are placed on the desk of the respondent's rostrum.

of the latter his own solution of the sophism he has constructed.

The following is the form of a divinity Act, with a specimen of the style of argumentation, as practised in the University of Cambridge. The compiler, in conformity with the principles laid down in the preceding part of this manual, has, at the bottom of the page, unfolded each argument in a categorical form.

The preliminaries of a divinity act, the formula of the prayers, the habit of the respondent, &c. are detailed in the " Ceremonies of the University of Cambridge," edited by H. Gunning, Esq.

Every one about to keep a divinity act first submits to the Regius Professor three or four questions, which should be on some important doctrine of the Christian religion, or leading article of the Protestant faith. The professor having selected one of these questions, the respondent (that is to be) makes it the subject of a Latin thesis: the delivery of which ought not to occupy more than half-an-hour.*

---

* The Church Articles supply suitable subjects for disputation. A good list of questions that have been already discussed is to be found in the Preface to Bishop Watson's Theological Tracts.

About ten days before the act is kept, the respondent should wait on the professor, in order to
obtain of him the second question. This is always
chosen exclusively by the professor himself, who,
when the disputation is ended, delivers a thesis
(called a *Determination*) upon it.   It is the province of the respondent to answer the arguments
brought against both questions.*

---

* It is greatly to be regretted, that many clergymen, after
entering on the public duties of their office, should often
neglect to cultivate the advantages conferred on them by a
University education.   Not that it is desirable, or even defensible, that a minister of the Gospel should employ much
of his time either in classical or philosophical researches;
but some familiarity with *theological* Greek and Latin might
fairly be expected of every divine, however arduous the duties of his parish may be.   It is incredible how much time
may be snatched for improvement out of the busiest and
most laborious life.   Erasmus wrote his "Praise of Folly,"
while travelling on horseback into Italy; "ne totum illud
tempus quo equo fuit insidendum, illiteratis fabulis terere-
tur."

No one who has discontinued for many years a moderate
cultivation of Greek and Latin, can proceed to the higher
degrees at the University, without disagreeable anticipations
of embarrassment and disgrace, in the attempt to hold a
public disputation.

The writings of Limborch may be very useful to any one
preparing for a divinity act.

On the professor having ascended his rostrum, he directs the respondent to begin: "Agas, Domine." The respondent then says, "Oremus," and pronounces the prayer "Actiones nostras," &c. He afterwards proposes the questions thus:

"*Quæstiones sunt: (exempli gratiâ:)*

1. '*Oblatio Christi semel facta perfecta redemptio est.*'

2. '*Fides justificans non potest à bonis operibus disjungi.*'"

As the question on which the respondent has composed his thesis is always proposed first, he then says, "De priori," and proceeds to deliver his thesis.

When the thesis is concluded, the first opponent is directed by the professor to ascend the rostrum: "Ascendat opponentium primus."

The opponent then reads the two questions, as the respondent had done before, and proceeds to his arguments.

To give as clear an idea as possible of the manner of opposing and responding, the discussion of the first argument is here exhibited in the form of dialogue.

OPPONENS.

Contra priorem.

1. Si Divus Paulus Christum appellet, "Agnum nostrum paschalem," cadit quæstio;

Sed Divus Paulus Christum appellat, "Agnum nostrum paschalem;"

Ergo cadit quæstio.

Provoco ad priorem Pauli Epist. ad Corinth. cap. 5to. com. 7mo.

RESPONDENS.

Concedo minorem, et nego consequentiam.

OPPONENS.

2. Si agnus paschalis non esset sacrificium piaculare, valet consequentia;

Sed agnus paschalis non erat sacrificium piaculare;

Ergo valet consequentia.

RESPONDENS.

Nego minorem.

OPPONENS.

Provoco ad Exodi cap. 12^{mum}. comm. 13^{tio}. et 14to. unde apparet sacrificium paschale primitùs institutum fuisse in id tantùm, ut, sanguine foribus asperso, angelus vindex domos Israëlitarum agnosceret, et illæsas præteriret; et in sæculis subsecutis observatum fuisse in id tantùm, ut majorum suorum ex Ægypto liberationem Judæi commemorarent.

Si dominus respondens nunc concedat minorem, necesse est consequentiam neget: et opponens pergit ad syllogismum tertium.

3. Si igitur neque mors Christi sit sacrificium piaculare, valent consequentia et argumentum ;

Sed igitur mors Christi non est sacrificium piaculare ;

Ergo valent consequentia et argumentum.

RESPONDENS.

Constat tum agni paschalis mactationem, tum Christi
mortem, fuisse reverà sacrificia. Hoc unum comparatio
ab Apostolo instituta requirit.   Esto, agni paschalis
mactationem nihil piaculare habuisse ; Christi tamen
mors, quippe quæ sacrificium sit, hactenùs agni paschalis mactationi respondet ; licet vim majorem habeat,
quia sacrificium est *piaculare*.

Si verò dominus respondens non concedat minorem in syllogismo secundo, tunc moderatoris
erit judicium suum interponere.   Si ille existimet
minorem valere, opponentem jubebit ad syllogismum
tertium pergere. Contra ea, si pronuntiet minorem
non valere, tunc domino opponenti nihil restat, nisi ut
det manus, et ad argumentum aliud novum pergat.

In hoc argumento dubitari potest, agni Paschalis
mactatio sacrificium piaculare fuerit, necne. Certè
sanguis foribus aspersus vim mali avertendi habuit,
ideòque effectum quendam piacularem. Sed agni
mactatio, in sæculis posterioribus quotannis repe-

tita, nullam aliam vim habere videtur nisi comme-
morativam.*

When the respondent has replied to the first
objection, the professor either signifies his approbation of the answer, or suggests another more appropriate and satisfactory. He then directs the
opponent to proceed to his next argument; "Pro-
bes aliter."

Second Argument.

OPPONENS.

1. Si doctrina de redemptione humanâ hoc funda-
mento nitatur, scilicet, necesse fuisse ut Divinæ justitiæ pro hominum peccatis satisfieret, cadit quæstio.

---

* The conditional syllogisms of which this objection
consists, correspond with the three propositions of a regular
categorical syllogism, and it may be viewed as *Celarent* with
the premises transposed; "Christ was the paschal lamb;
the paschal lamb was not a piacular sacrifice; therefore
Christ was not a piacular sacrifice."

Ce- The paschal lamb was not a piacular sacrifice;
-la- Christ was the paschal lamb; therefore
-rent. Christ was not a piacular sacrifice.

In the major proposition, the middle term (the paschal
lamb) is used in its primary and literal sense; in the minor
proposition, in its secondary and metaphorical sense. It is
not, therefore, fairly compared with the terms of the conclusion or question. This is, "Fallacia æquivocationis."
After all, the truth of the major proposition admits of
doubt.

Sed doctrina de redemptione humanâ hoc funda-
mento nititur ;

Ergo cadit quæstio.

2. Si, ut hoc efficeretur, pœnæ peccatis humanis
debitæ in Christum translatæ fuerint,—unum inter
omnes à peccati labe purum, valet consequentia.

Sed, ut hoc efficeretur, &c.

Ergo valet consequentia.

Provoco ad Esaiæ cap. 53^{tium.} com. 6to. et ad priorem
Petri Epistolam, cap. 2do. com. 24to.

3. Si verò justitiæ proprium sit, pœnas non nisi de
nocentibus exigere, valent consequentia et argumentum.

Sed justitiæ proprium est, &c.

Ergo valent consequentia et argumentum.*

---

* The punishment of the innocent for the guilty, says
the opponent, being repugnant to the principles of justice,
could not have satisfied Divine justice for the sins of men.
The innocence and vicarious punishment of Christ being
supposed to be conceded, the objection, stated in form, will
appear thus :

Ce- What is irreconcileable with justice, cannot sa-
     tisfy Divine justice.

-la- To inflict the punishment of guilt on the innocent,
      is irreconcileable with justice ; therefore

-rent. It could not satisfy Divine justice.

Under the moral government which God exercises here,
the innocent very frequently suffer for the guilty. If, then,
we allow the moral government and attributes of God, vicarious punishment and the Divine justice will no longer be

K

Responsum.

E Sacris Scripturis hoc unum colligendum est de redemptione humanâ; scilicet Christi mortem hunc
effectum habuisse, ut homines à peccati pœnâ libe-
raret. Quod rationi satis consentaneum est. Vi-
demus enim rerum naturam à Divino Opifice et Rec-
tore ita constitutam, ut plurima nobis contingant bene-
ficia aliorum ope, qui sæpe incommoda volentes subeunt,
in id tantùm ut nos adjuvent. Nihil igitur objici potest
contra doctrinam de redemptione humanâ in Sacris
Scripturis traditam, quod non pari jure contra quoti-
dianum rerum humanarum et Divinæ providentiæ
ordinem adhibeatur.

Third Argument.

1. Si Divus Paulus doceat cœnam Dominicam idem
esse Christianis quod epulæ sacrificales tum Judæis
tum Ethnicis, cadit quæstio.
Sed Divus Paulus docet, &c.
Ergo cadit quæstio.
Provoco ad 1 Cor. x. 16—21.

2. Si igitur cœna Domini sit epulum ex oblatis, valet
consequentia.
Sed cœna Domini est, &c.
Ergo valet consequentia.

---

considered incompatible. The minor premiss of the categorical syllogism will be denied, in this case, to be universally true.

3. Si igitur oblatio Christi sæpiùs repetatur, valent consequentia et argumentum.

Sed oblatio Christi, &c.

Ergo valent consequentia et argumentum.*

---

* This argument may be stated categorically, thus, in three syllogisms.

1.

Bar- What a sacrificial feast was to the Jews and Heathens, is what the Lord's Supper is to Christians;

-ba- A feast upon propitiatory offerings is what a sacrificial feast was to the Jews and Heathens; therefore

-ra. A feast upon propitiatory offerings is what the Lord's
Supper is to Christians.

2.

Bar- A Christian propitiatory offering is the oblation of
Christ;

-ba- What takes place in the Lord's Supper is a Christian propitiatory offering; therefore

-ra. What takes place in the Lord's Supper, is the oblation of Christ.

3.

Bar- What takes place in the Lord's Supper is frequently
repeated;

-ba- The propitiatory oblation of Christ is what takes
place in the Lord's Supper; therefore

-ra. It is frequently repeated.

The middle term of the first syllogism is here taken in different senses in the major and minor premiss. In the major premiss, it means what a sacrificial feast was, *with regard to one particular*, (viz. communion with the Deity,)

Responsum.

Non docet Paulus cœnam Dominicam *prorsus* idem esse Christianis quod Judæis atque Ethnicis Epulæ sacrificales. Affirmat quandam esse similitudinem, et hâc tantùm parte, quòd insit utrique sacrificantium communicatio cum numine. Nec comparatio arctiùs premenda est. Apostolus non affirmat Christianos, in Eucharistiâ celebrandâ, et Ethnicos, in Epulis sacrificalibus, in hoc similiter agere, quòd oblatis vescantur; sed quòd et Christiani vero cum Deo, et Ethnici cum idolis suis, religiosam communicationem instituant.

Fourth Argument.

This and the following argument are against the second question, according to the rules for keeping a first opponency.

Contra Secundam.

1. Si fides justificationem antecedat, cadit quæstio.
Sed fides justificationem antecedit;
Ergo cadit quæstio.

2. Si opera qualiacunque ante justificationem peracta rationem peccati habeant, valet consequentia.

---

and thus, in *that* particular, it agrees with the major term; in the minor premiss, it is taken simply, and thus, in *another* particular, (viz. its propitiatory character,) it agrees with the minor term. It is not, therefore, fairly compared with the terms of the conclusion. This may be referred to "Fallacia à dicto secundum quid, ad dictum simpliciter."

Sed opera qualiacunque, &c.

Ergo valet consequentia.

3. Si igitur fides quà justificationem consequimur, existere possit à bonis operibus disjuncta, valent consequentia et argumentum.

Sed fides quâ, &c.

Ergo valent consequentia et argumentum.*

---

* The opponent contends, that as justifying faith precedes justification, and all works before justification are sinful, therefore justifying faith may exist apart from good works.   The formal statement of this argument requires four categorical syllogisms.

1.

Ce-   Works that have in them the nature of sin are not
        good works ;

-la-   All works done before justification have in them
        the nature of sin ; therefore

-rent. No works done before justification are good works.

2.

Bar- Whatever is preceded by justification is preceded
        by what precedes justification ;

-ba- Good works are preceded by justification ; therefore

-ra.   They are preceded by what precedes justification.

3.

Bar- What precedes justification precedes good works.
        (*Equipollent to the conclusion of the last.*)

-ba- Faith precedes justification ; therefore

-ra.   It precedes good works.

Responsum.

Cogitatione solâ distingui possunt fides et opera bona. Fides fons est, opera bona sunt fluenta; fides causa, opera bona effectus. Simul ac fides existat, justificatio incipit, nullâque morâ interpositâ, subsequuntur opera bona. Ut sol igitur ante radios solares, ita fides ante opera bona; sed fide existente, opera bona proveniant necesse est. Neque magis disjungi possunt à fide, quàm lux à sole.

Fifth Argument.

1. Si operanti merces tribuatur non ex gratiâ sed ex debito, cadit quæstio.

Sed operanti merces, &c.

Ergo cadit quæstio.

Provoco ad Rom. iv. 4.

4.

Bar- Whatever precedes good works is distinct from them ;

-ba- Justifying faith precedes good works ; therefore

-ra. It is distinct from them.

Faith may be separated from good works only in thought. Faith is the fountain-head ; good works, the streams that flow from it. Faith is the cause ; good works, the effect. As soon as there is faith, justification begins, and good works immediately follow. As, therefore, the sun must have existed before the sunbeams, so faith must be previous to good works. But if there be faith, good works are of necessity produced; nor can they any more be separated from faith, than light can be parted from the sun.

2. Si verò justificatio, quam per fidem consequimur, sit ex gratiâ, valet consequentia.

Sed justificatio, &c.

Ergo valet consequentia.

Provoco ad Rom. iv. 5.

3. Si igitur opera bona, cum eâ, quâ justificamur, fide nihil commune habeant, valent consequentia et argumentum.

Sed opera bona, &c.

Ergo valent consequentia et argumentum.*

---

* The reward of him who works, says the opponent, is shewn in Scripture to be not of grace, but of debt. But *our* reward, viz. Justification by faith, is proved by Scripture to be of grace; therefore it cannot be the reward of him who works, nor is justifying faith connected with good works. This argument, in order to be formally stated, requires, like the last, four categorical syllogisms.

1.

Ce-   That which is of debt is not of grace;

-la-   The reward of him who works is of debt; therefore

-rent. It is not of grace.

2.

Ce-   What is of grace, is not the reward of him who works.

(Converse of the conclusion of the last syllogism, E.)

-la-   Justification by faith is of grace; therefore

-rent. It is not the reward of him who works.

Responsum.

Fatendum est, justificationem nostram Divinâ ex gratiâ solummodò concessam esse; non autem sequi-

---

3.

Ce- What is not the reward of him who works, has no connexion with good works;

Predicate.

-la- Justification by faith is ‾not-the-reward-of-him- who-works; therefore

-rent. It has no connexion with good works.

4.

Ce- The instrumental cause of justification has no more connexion with good works, than justification itself has;

la- Justifying faith is the instrumental cause of justification; therefore

-rent. It has no more connexion with good works than justification itself has.

The major proposition of the third syllogism is unduly assumed. That which is not the reward of works may yet have connexion with them *in other respects.* Though justification is a favour, not a reward of works, yet works may be required as a *condition* of justification; and in this respect they may be inseparably connected. This circumstance does not diminish our debt of gratitude to God, to whose grace, as the efficient cause, all spiritual blessings are ascribable.

They who object to call good works, "Conditions of salvation," may term them, the necessary fruits of the faith whereby we obtain salvation; although salvation itself must be accounted a gratuitous benefit of God.

tur, licet bona opera pro causâ justificationis non ha-
benda sint, nihil esse inter fidem et bona opera commune. Fieri enim potest, quod Sacræ Scripturæ reverà
docent, ut opera bona sint *conditiones* salutis, quam
tamen Divinæ gratiæ, quasi causæ efficienti, acceptam
referre debemus.

Si nolis opera bona *conditiones* salutis appellari, tunc
ea licet appelles, fructus necessarios fidei illius quâ
salutem consequimur ; cùm tamen salus ipsa sit Dei
beneficium gratuitum.

The opponent, when his last argument has been
answered by the respondent, descends from the
rostrum upon the moderator thus dismissing him ;
" Satis disputâsti."

ACTS IN THE CIVIL LAW.

Before keeping an Act in the Civil Law, the
student submits, to the Regius Professor in that
faculty, a few questions, that he may fix on one of
them as a fit subject for a Latin thesis.*

---

* A candidate for the degree of LL.B. must submit to
the Professor the question he means to write upon, at least
one term before the act is kept. A candidate for the degree of LL.D. must do the same at least two terms previously to his act.

A second question is also chosen by the professor exclusively, who reads a Determination on it, when the disputation is finished.

On the day of the exercise, the respondent having occupied his rostrum, and the professor being seated, the Father of the respondent's college directs him to begin: " Domine respondens, agas."

The following is a copy of the printed questions proposed by the Professor in his examination paper of the present year. Other questions in MS. are also given to each student, according to the nature of the subjects proposed for discussion in the Schools.

1. Explain the nature and utility of syllogisms in general.

2. Explain the nature of the syllogisms used in the law schools.

3. State an instance of a Dilemma in favour of your first question from

4. Prove your first question to be true by Induction from

5. Form an argument in two hypothetical syllogisms, in favour of your first question, from

. 6. Form, in Latin, an argument in three hypothetical syllogisms, against your first question, from

7. Form, in Latin, an argument against your second question, in three hypothetical syllogisms, from

Let the minor of the second syllogism be false.

8. Make a short statement, in *English*, of your first question.

9. Make a short statement, in *Latin*, of your second question.

The respondent then proposes the questions, placing that first on which his thesis is written.

Except when an opponency is kept for a Doctor's degree, the Regius Professor is himself both opponent and moderator. He produces as many arguments against each question as he thinks proper, in the form of syllogism already explained.

It is the office of the respondent (as in the Divinity School) to defend each question by an appropriate answer to the objections adduced by the opponent.

If the answer of the respondent be satisfactory to the professor, he signifies his approbation, and proceeds, in the capacity of opponent, to propose his next argument.   But if the answer of the respondent be erroneous or inconclusive, the professor (departing for the time from the character of opponent) points out to the respondent the true solution of the difficulty: and this he does, not only for the advantage of the respondent but, for the instruction of the auditors frequenting the law-school, the majority of whom attend there expressly with a view to prepare themselves for responding in a disputation.

In the course of the act, the professor, at his discretion, tries the ability of the respondent, by interrogatories on such subjects as are connected with the question.

The following is a specimen of the nature of the questions discussed, and of the manner of arguing against them. The student may easily collect, from the references,* the nature and force of the argu-

Quæstiones sunt:

1. *Decemviri creditoribus in debitores jus vitæ atque necis non dederunt.*

2. *Romani primos Christianos non ideò persecuti sunt, quia cœtus nocturnos celebrabant.*

Contra priorem.

1. Si in lege Decemvirali de debitore, pœna capitis non nisi de ultimo supplicio est accipienda, cadit quæstio.

Sed in lege Decemvirali, &c.

Ergo cadit quæstio.

2. Si dominis in servos jus erat vitæ atque necis, valet minor.

---

* A copy of the *Corpus Juris Civilis*, is placed on the rostrum of the respondent, and another on that of the opponent.

Sed dominis in servos, &c.

Ergo valet minor.

3. Si æris convicti jure Decemvirali in servitutem redigebantur, valent consequentia et argumentum.

Sed æris convicti, &e.

Ergo valent consequentia et argumentum.

The opponent then refers the respondent to the following authorities in confirmation of his argument, and it is the duty of the respondent to make his answer.

Ins. 1. 8. 1.

D. 1. 5. 5.

Matt. 18. 25.

Liv. Hist. 6. 14.

Contra alteram.

1. Si causa persecutionum quibus primi Christiani vexabantur, aut ab ipsâ Christi religione aut ex quâdam ratione civili petenda est, cadit quæstio.

Sed causa persecutionum, &c.

Ergo cadit quæstio.

2. Si Romani omnibus ferè gentibus suam religionem et suos ritus celebrare permitterent, valet consequentia.

Sed Romani, &c.

Ergo valet consequentia.

3. Si igitur necesse est ut quædam ratio civilis eos excitaret ad Christianos vexandos, valet eonsequentia.

Sed necesse est ut, &c.

Ergo valet consequentia.

4. Si ista ratio fuit metus ne quid detrimenti caperet respublica, valent consequentia et argumentum.

Sed ista ratio fuit, &c.
Ergo valent consequentia et argumentum.

> Tac. Annal. 1, 73.
> xii. Tab.
> Leg. Gab.
> SCT Marc.
> D. 47, 22, 1.
> D. 47, 11, 2.

In the progress of this argument, the opponent might, if occasion required, refer to the sacred Scripture, as well as to the authorities above mentioned.

The respondent's answer will be suggested partly from his own interpretation of these authorities cited by the opponent, and partly from his own view of the question in general.

ACTS IN MEDICINE.

A medical thesis may be composed on any practical, physiological, or pathological question. It must be of such a length as not to consume more than half-an-hour in the delivery.

For the degree of M. B. the question must be submitted to the professor, for his approval, six weeks before the act is kept; and, for the degree of M. D., three months before.

The respondent has to defend two questions, of which one is appointed exclusively by the professor; as in the case of a Divinity Act.

The professor does not restrict the opponent from extending the number of his arguments, if he pleases; but he must not produce fewer than five in all; *i. e.* three against the first question, and two against the second. Each of these arguments may consist of two, three, or four syllogisms.

There is but one opponent; and if the act be kept for a Doctor's degree, the opponent is most frequently the professor himself.

The forms of keeping an act in Medicine, correspond with those observed in keeping an act in the civil law.

In a medical disputation, it does not always happen that the respondent maintains the position which the moderator holds to be true.   The truth may appear on the opponent's side, and the decision be accordingly given in his favour. The following, however, are specimens in which the position maintained is true, and the objections fallacious.

Quæstiones sunt:

1. *Venæsectio primum et præcipuum remedium est Enteritidis.*

2. *Bilis è sanguine venoso secernitur.*

OPPONENS.

Contra priorem.

1. Si intestinorum inflammatio ab alvo diu astrictâ et suppressâ sæpe oriatur, cadit quæstio.

Sed intestinorum &c. sæpe oritur;

Ergo cadit quæstio.

RESPONDENS.

Concedo intestinorum inflammationem cum alvo diu astrictâ sæpiùs conjunctam esse, et aliquando ex hac origine exortam.

OPPONENS.

2. Si alvum solvere et purgare primum et præcipuum sit hujus mali remedium, valet consequentia.

Sed alvum solvere, &c.

Ergo valet consequentia.

RESPONDENS.

Concedo quoque maximi esse momenti ut alvus astricta solvatur.

OPPONENS.

3. Si igitur intestinorum inflammatio ab alvo astrictâ orta, optimè curetur medicamentis purgantibus, valent consequentia et argumentum.

Sed intestinorum inflammatio, &c.

Ergo valent consequentia et argumentum.

RESPONDENS.

In hoc morbo res maximi momenti est ut depellatur inflammatio, id quod optimè per venæsectionem efficitur. Animadvertendum quoque medicamenta purgantia sæpe vim suam non exerere, nisi post detractionem sanguinis.

OPPONENS.

Contra alteram.

1. Si in omni aliâ glandulâ corporis, præterquam hepate, secretio humoris fiat è sanguine arterioso, cadit quæstio.

Sed in omni &c.

Ergo cadit quæstio.

RESPONDENS.

Concedo minorem et nego consequentiam.

OPPONENS.

2. Si in rebus obscuris investigandis confidere necesse sit comparationi similitudinis vel analogiæ, valet consequentia.

Sed in rebus obscuris &c.

Ergo valet consequentia.

RESPONDENS.

Concedo minorem &c.

OPPONENS.

3. Si igitur ab hac comparatione concludendum sit, ut bilis è sanguine arterioso secernatur, valent consequentia et argumentum.

Sed ab hac comparatione &c.

Ergo valent consequentia et argumentum.

L

RESPONDENS.

Argumento domini opponentis refragatur quidem analogia, quum jecori, quod bilem secernit, sanguis venosus suppeditetur, (ex Venâ Portârum scilicet,) simili modo quo cæteris glandulis sanguis arteriosus, ex arteriis suis.

ACTS IN THE SCHOOL OF ARTS.

The Preliminaries of these Acts are, of necessity, well known to all who are concerned in keeping them. No one can oppose or respond in the School of Arts, till he has resided seven Terms in the University. A particular introduction to the following questions would, therefore, be superfluous.

Quæstiones sunt:

1. *Rectè statuit Newtonus in nonâ suâ sectione libri primi.*

2. *Rectè sese habent Principia Calculi tum Differentialis tum Integralis.*

3. *Rectè statuit Paleius de Virtute.*

Contra primam.

1. Si cùm spiralis reciproca in antecedentia revolvatur eâdem velocitate angulari quâ corpus in consequentia movetur, orbita in fixo spatio descripta fiat

linea recta in quâ corpus motu uniformi ad centrum accedit, cadit quæstio.

Sed cùm &c. **** fit &c. *** accedit;

Ergo cadit quæstio.

2. Si cùm vis in spirali reciprocâ varietur $\frac{1}{D^3}$, et virium differentia in orbitâ quiescente et in orbitâ in fixo spatio descriptâ varietur similiter $\frac{1}{D^3}$, consequens sit totam vim in orbitâ in fixo spatio descriptâ variari $\frac{1}{D^3}$, valet consequentia.

Sed cùm vis, &c. **** consequens est &c.

Ergo valet consequentia.

3. Si verò cùm vis varietur $\frac{1}{D^3}$, corpus nequeat in rectâ lineâ ad centrum descendere motu uniformi, valent consequentia et argumentum.

Sed cùm &c. **** nequit &c.

Ergo valent consequentia et argumentum.

RESPONSUM.

Differentia virium centripetarum et centrifugarum in orbitâ in fixo spatio descriptâ, eadem est ac in orbitâ quiescente. Sed in spirali reciprocâ vires centripeta et centrifuga æquales sunt. Ergo in rectâ lineâ quæ in fixo spatio describitur æquales sunt; ideòque corpus nullâ vi impulsum velocitate primâ ad centrum uniformiter accedit.

The first opponent produces two other similar arguments against the first question.

Contra secundam.

1. Si inter limites $x=a$, $x=b$ $\int \frac{dx}{x}$ fiat $h. l. \frac{a}{b}$, cadit quæstio.

Sed inter limites &c.

Ergo cadit quæstio.

2. Si inter eosdem limites $\int x^{n-1}\, dx$ fiat $\frac{a^n - b^n}{n}$ valet consequentia.

Sed inter &c.

Ergo valet consequentia.

3. Si igitur cùm $n = o$, $\int \frac{dx}{x}$ fiat $\frac{a^o - b^o}{o}$, seu $\frac{1-1}{o}$, seu o, valent consequentia et argumentum.

Sed cùm &c.

Ergo valent consequentia et argumentum.

RESPONSUM.

$$a^n = 1 + h.\, l.\, a.\, n + \overline{\frac{h.\, l.\, a.}{1\,.\,2}}\Big)^2\, n^2 + \&c.$$

$$b^n = 1 + h.\, l.\, b.\, n + \overline{\frac{h.\, l.\, b.}{1\,.\,2}}\Big)^2\, n^2 + \&c.$$

$$\therefore a^n - b^n = \Big\{ h.\, l.\, a - h.\, l.\, b \Big\} .\, n + \&c.$$

$$\therefore \frac{a^n - b^n}{h} = \Big\{ h.l.\,a - h.l.\,b \Big\} + \frac{\overline{h.l.\,a}\,)^2 - \overline{h.l.\,b}\,)^2}{1\,.\,2} n + \&c.$$

$$\therefore \frac{a^o - b^o}{o} = h.\, l.\, a - h.\, l.\, b.$$

$$= h.\, l.\, \frac{a}{b}$$

Ergo valor fractionis $\frac{a^n - b^n}{n}$ cum $n = o$ non evanescit, sed fit $h.\,l.\,\frac{a}{b}$ ideòque nulla discrepantia existit.

The first opponent produces one other similar argument against this question.

Contra tertiam.

1. Si Dei voluntas sit virtutis regula, cadit quæstio.
Sed Dei voluntas est, &c.
Ergo cadit quæstio.

2. Si Dei voluntas ideò nos astringat quia præmia
pænæque vitæ futuræ ex Dei arbitrio pendent, valet
consequentia.
Sed Dei voluntas &c.
Ergo valet consequentia.

3. Si igitur, posito quòd angelorum malorum princeps summo rerum imperio potitus esset, voluntas
ejus nos pari jure astringeret, valent consequentia et
argumentum.
Sed, posito quòd &c.
Ergo valent consequentia et argumentum.

Responsum.

Ut alia taceam, Deus homines felices vult; angelorum malorum princeps, miseros; huic ut resistamus,
illi ut obediamus, ratio et natura suadent. Priusquam
angelorum malorum princeps hominum felicitatem
velle possit, naturam suam se exuat necesse est.

Against the third question one argument only
is produced.

FINIS.

HENRY G. BOHN,

NOW OF

No. 4, YORK STREET, COVENT GARDEN,

HAS JUST PUBLISHED

A CATALOGUE

OF

A VERY CHOICE COLLECTION OF BOOKS,

ENGLISH AND FOREIGN,

Partly selected during an extensive tour on the Continent, partly from fine private libraries in this country: the whole offered at very moderate prices. The. Catalogue comprehends above 4,000 articles of the first quality, in every department of literature, especially the fine arts, divinity, classics, and rare books, a great portion of them in rich old morocco bindings by De Rome, Desseuil, and Padeloup. Among the black letter and Aldine editions are many that have never before been heard of, and the Spanish collection is the best in this country. The price of the catalogue is 3s., but gentlemen sending their names, and the country trade applying free of postage, may obtain it gratis. It is particularly requested that the address be observed.

CPSIA information can be obtained
at www.ICGtesting.com
Printed in the USA
BVOW06*1716261017
498733BV00011B/400/P